RAISED BED GARDENING
FOR BEGINNERS

EXPERTLY MAXIMIZE EVERY SQUARE INCH OF YOUR GARDENING SPACE AND ENSURE HIGH PRODUCE YIELDS

BY
TOM GREER

Table of Contents

Introduction

The movement to cities has meant that people are increasingly getting disconnected from their roots. They are getting away from nature, and many people feel that void inside them. There is always a longing to stay close to nature, and gardening is the perfect way to do that. However, limitations of space and time are a few things that can make you feel restrained. You may feel that there is not enough space to allow your porch to look spacious and beautiful, and it may hinder you from planting the trees you've always loved. This can be a dream that can easily be fulfilled with the help of raised bed gardening.

Raised bed gardening is a great concept that can help you have greenery all around you without having to bend, till, and operate heavy tools. It can help you grow plants without deteriorating the aesthetic appeal of your property. On the contrary, raised bed gardening can help in increasing the visual appeal of the property several times over.

It is a simple gardening technique that will not only allow you to grow better plants that you couldn't have grown in the present soil conditions, but it will also help you in getting a better yield from limited growth.

Although the initial preparation required for raised bed gardening is high, it is an easy way to manage your garden. It eliminates a lot of restrictions that may have made gardening a distant dream for you. Even if you have easy mobility issues or find bending over difficult, raised bed gardening provides an easy solution for all the problems.

This book will provide you with all the information required to carry out raised bed gardening on your own. It will prove to be an easy-to-follow book that can make gardening easy for you.

To get the most out of this book, you must give it a thorough read and plan all the parts carefully. The execution part would span over a very long period, but the preparation must be done in advance. This book will help you in chalking out such a plan.

It is not uncommon for people to fear gardening as they believe that it requires a lot of hard work. This book clears all the myths and clearly explains the things you'd need to do and things you can stop worrying about.

We hope that you will be able to benefit from this book and lead a healthy and fulfilling life!

1. Take Your Garden to a Higher Level: Above-Ground Gardening in Containers, Raised Beds, and Vertical Gardens

Get your tools ready, gear up, and let's get to make a raised bed. First, we need to know the different kinds of raised beds that we can choose from according to our space and what materials we can use (usually these spare materials are already present in our garage). After getting all the knowledge regarding the whereabouts of the making, we will get down to business, i.e., building our very own raised bed.

Raised beds are a great expansion to any lawn garden in the event that you have space and materials required. Raised bed gardens are one of the most beneficial approaches to developing your own food. They give you better access to your garden's soil conditions and take into consideration small and simple areas for your yields to grow. Raised beds can be simple or very detailed, relying upon your necessities and the general taste you wish to make them in. Utilize the data below to figure out what sort of raised beds you might want in your nursery.

Raised bed gardening is a straightforward method that can improve the well-being and profitability of your nursery. Raised beds have better soil structure and seepage, permitting our soil to heat up prior to the season, and giving you a head start on spring. Weeding can be to a lesser degree of an issue in raised beds than in other different plant gardens. Following are the different types of raised beds available for you to choose from according to your likeness:

Raised Ground Beds

The least sophisticated type of raised bed is level topped hills, generally 6–8-inch high. They require no extra materials other than an excessive amount of soil. Use excess soil to frame the beds or do it in 3–4 crawls of soil from pathways between beds. If you use the extra soil mentioned above, be confident that it does not originate from a territory where soil-borne plant microbes or harmful chemicals such as lead and pesticides are available, as they are not suitable for the plants; they accumulate in the plant cells and destroy them by spreading different plant diseases. Regardless of whether you uncover your pathways or not, keep the entrance zones around the raised beds at a rate of 24-inch wide from each other.

Firstly, it is advised to choose according to the size of your raised ground bed. If by any means, you can arrive at just one side of the bed, the most extreme width should be 2 ½ feet and not more to save space for other beds. If the case is such that you can reach the bed from both sides, the bed can be up to 5 feet wide. Length and shape are all together up to you; make it any way you like according to the space that is available to you.

As the season proceeds further, the soil will settle down, yet the hill in the bed will remain. Raised ground beds, once made, need just minor reshaping towards the beginning of each season. Each season adds in natural compost to the surface as mulch during the developing season or after the harvesting. Night crawlers and other soil living beings will bring it down into the soil, so better care should be given to the soil.

Containerized Raised Beds

A raised bed with 10–12-inch dividers offers more insurance to plants in high-traffic zones close to walkways and roads. In traffic-free zones where the reflected heat may pressurize the plants, raising a bed to a couple of feet can reduce heat provided to the plant, hence helping in their growth. These beds with much higher dividers boost plant growth and reduce maintenance in such areas. For most wheelchair users, 27-inch is excellent working tallness, yet you can custom-form the beds to any stature you may prefer. Pick the width to coordinate with your arm's length.

To make a raised bed 27-inch high, place 1 2-by-4-inch and 3 2-by-8-inch sheets on a flat plane, with 2-by-4-inch loads up vertically, particularly at the corners. Use decking screws to attach the vertical strengthening sheets and to join the corners. You can make a sitting edge by attaching a 1-by-4-inch board level on the edge, broadening it over the sides. Fill in the bed just made with a blend of soil and natural organic matter, and add 2–4-inch of soil again every year as the soil settles in and grows old. Take care of your beds, and keep watering them on a regular basis, eventually to grow your plants beautifully.

Vertical Gardening

What vertical gardening does, is that it utilizes space that would otherwise have been lost to the gardener. It is very useful if you have a walled garden or even just a bare wall that would provide you somewhere to hang your containers. It is an excellent method for gaining extra capacity where space is at a premium, and the apartment patio is the perfect example. What the wall does is provide support for whatever hanging garden system you opt for. You increase your growing area and, at the same time, you turn what might have been a bland or even ugly wall into something of abundant beauty. This system really can provide the gardener with some stunning results and can be used for edible crops or ornamental ones or perhaps a combination of the 2.

2.   If I Had a Hammer: How to Construct a Raised Bed

Although there are many materials you can build your raised beds out of, most people will use wood, at least for their first few beds, purely due to availability and simplicity. This is a good starting point, and you can obviously adjust the size of the wood according to the size of the bed you are building.

A lot of people prefer wood because it allows you to easily fix things to the bed such as netting, fleece, or cover it with black plastic over winter. The staple gun will become your friend as you attach extras to your beds as and when you need them.

Hopefully, you will have planned out your garden and know how many raised beds you need to build and of what size. From this, you can determine the amount of wood that you need.

Choose wood. We are using 12-inch wide planks so that we get a good depth of soil. You can use 8-inch planks if you prefer for beds that aren't as high.

The Materials You Will Need

*   4-by-16-inch-long 4 by 4's (the corner posts)

- 2-by-4-foot-long 2 by 12's (the bed ends)

- 2-by-8-foot-long 2 by 12's (the bed sides)

- 24-by-3.5-inch #14 decking screws

- 16 cubic feet of planting soil

- 16 cubic feet of compost

The soil and compost are a good start, but feel free to mix compost with soil, manure, horticultural sand, and so on to get the right planting mix for your bed. I tend to mix all 4 together, so I get good drainage and rich soil that ensures strong plant growth.

These are optional materials if you want to protect your bed from birds and burrowing pests. These are used to build a cage over your bed to prevent pests from getting into your plants, ideal for fruit bushes or brassicas, which can be devastated by caterpillars:

- 24-by-0.5-inch #8 decking screws

- 6-by-12-inch long pieces of ½-inch PVC pipes

- 3-by-10-foot long pieces of ⅜ gauge rebar

- 3-by-3-by-5-foot rolls of ¼-inch hardwire mesh (to prevent burrowing animals)

- 12-by-1-inch galvanized tube straps

- 1 roll bird netting

- Drip watering system

The Tools You Will Need

- Drill

- 5/32-inch drill bit (for pilot holes for the decking screws)

- Ruler

- Pencil

- Shovel/trowel

- Level

- Staple gun (optional)

- Wire cutters (optional)

- Gloves

- 2-by-12-inch adjustable woodworking bar clamps (optional)

- 2-by-6-foot adjustable woodworking bar clamps (optional)

The Frame

You will need to work on a flat surface for this and will build it upside down. Place 1 of the 4-foot-long 2-by-12 edging boards on its narrow side and place 1 of the 4-by-4 uprights flush with the end of the board. Use a friend or a woodworking clamp to keep this in place.

Pre-drill 3 evenly spaced pilot holes along the post to attach it; this prevents the board from splitting. Use 3 (½-inch) screws to secure the board to the post and then remove the woodworking clamp.

The picture above shows you what you are trying to achieve. Both long boards are screwed (or nailed in this case) to the corner post. You can see that one of the long boards rests against the other to provide a more solid joint. Screw the 2 long boards together on the ends here if you want to provide the structure with a little bit more rigidity.

Repeat the process until you have built a rectangle, making sure the boards are flush with the corner posts and each other. Pre-drill the holes before drilling to the proper size and screw all the boards together firmly. I'd recommend an electric screwdriver as it will save a lot of time and effort! Now you should have your rectangular bed.

The Paths

You will need to leave paths between the beds that are about a wheelbarrow's width (or wider if required for a wheelchair). These cannot be left as soil as you will get weeds growing, which will invade your beds and give you extra work to do. The soil will also get very wet and waterlogged, making access harder during inclement weather.

Dig over the paths, remove any weeds, and then tamp down the soil. Cover it with a good quality weed membrane and then cover that with 3–4-inch of bark, as you can see in the picture above. If you prefer, you can put down slabs, bricks, or paving, but it needs to be something you can walk on easily or push your wheelchair down. It must keep the weeds down and prevent them from establishing themselves. Use a high-quality weed membrane as the cheaper ones will allow weeds to grow through. Some people just use the weed membrane as a path because it takes away the work of replacing the bark chips every few years.

Positioning and Anchoring

You are going to need a friend to help you move the bed now, so turn it the right way up and move it to the position where it will be sited. Orientating it north/south will maximize the amount of sun your plants will get, but it isn't necessary.

Ensure the area where you are placing the raised beds is level. It doesn't have to be precise but must be mostly level. If it isn't, then you end up with gaps at the bottom of your bed, which allows the soil to escape onto your paths and weeds to invade.

Where each corner post will be located, dig a hole about 6-inch deep and sink the post into the ground. Depending on your soil, you may find it very difficult to push the corner posts into the soil. The small hole will help secure the bed and get it flush with the soil.

Next, you need to ensure that the bed is level on all sides as this will help with drainage and ensure it looks neat. A bed that isn't level will look odd (I've inherited a few that aren't), and they will play on your mind! Uneven beds also mean that water will run off or pool on one side rather than be evenly distributed. Lay a long board over your raised bed and put your spirit level on it to check how level it is; then proceed to adjust the depth of the corners until the bed is level. You will want to do this along the diagonals, ideally. Once the bed is level, then you can backfill the post holes and compact the soil.

Keep the Birds Out

As an optional step, you can build a frame that you can use to either put up bird netting or fleece to protect your plants from birds, airborne pests, and winter. If you are doing this, then you need to do it now before you put the soil in the bed as you are fixing these to the inside of the beds.

On the inside of the long sides, evenly space 3 of the 12-inch pieces of ½-inch PVC pipe in an upright position. Once you have

25

done this on one side, you need to repeat the process on the other long side, ensuring that the pipes on this side are in the same position as those on the other. These are the support tubes for the hoops.

Use 2 tube straps and secure each PVC pipe in an upright position to the bed using 2 (½-inch) screws for each strap.

The ⅜-inch gauge rebar needs to be bent into a half-circle, with each end placed in the PVC pipe support, which will form the hoop for the netting. This step is best done once the bed is filled with soil, so you don't knock the hoops. For further stability, you can screw the rebar into the PVC pipe.

As an alternative, you can just use plastic pipes. I have used, as a temporary solution, canes with plant pots on the ends and netting stapled to the raised bed. There's a lot of different ways you can do this and many which can cost you very little time and money.

Keeping Out Burrowing Pests

If you live in an area with gophers, moles, or other burrowing pests, then you need to put the hardware cloth, a very tight wire mesh, in the bottom of the bed before you fill it. This will stop the pests from coming up underneath your plants and ruining your crops. You can use a tight mesh chicken wire or something similar which may be cheaper.

Rake the soil until it is leveled and then carefully flatten it down. Wear gloves to protect your hands and line the bottom of the bed with the hardware cloth, curving it up slightly, so it touches the side of the bed. Make sure the wire is flat, and then, using your staple gun, staple it to the sides of the bed. Use wire cutters to trim it to size and remove any sharp edges, so you don't cut yourself when digging in the bed.

Adding the Soil

Fill the bed with your chosen soil mix and compact it gently, then rake the soil smooth and wet it a little with your garden hose. Soil and compost are cheaper if you are buying them in bulk rather than by the bag.

Don't compact the soil too much, but you need to compact it enough that your plants will be secure when put in the soil. If the soil is too loose, then the plants will blow over and end up uprooted. If the soil is too compacted, then you will find it harder to plant and weed.

The soil level will settle in the first year, so be prepared to top the bed up either partway through the growing season or at the end of the year. If you have used manure on the bed, then this will rot down, and the soil level will also drop. I tend to top dress my beds with manure every winter, cover them, and it has usually broken down by spring.

If you are planning in advance, then you can fill the beds with manure. When using fresh manure, it will need 6–12 months to rot down fully, cover it, and add worms to speed up the process.

Well-rotted manure will need less time to break down, depending on how rotten it is.

Setting Up Irrigation

If you are going to add an irrigation system, then set that up now and put it in place. This is easiest to do before any plants are in place. For a bed of this size, you can use ¼-inch emitter lines spaced 1 foot apart.

And that is your first raised bed built. It isn't too difficult to do, and anyone can build one very easily, even I can manage it! Obviously, you can adjust the size of the wooden planks depending on the size of the bed you are building, but the principles remain the same.

If you haven't got access to electricity at your vegetable plot, then I recommend cutting the wood to size at home using power tools. Build the beds at your vegetable plot using a battery-powered drill and screwdriver. Depending on the wood you are using, it can be very hard work cutting and screwing the wood together by hand. Use a cordless drill that has plenty of power, ideally at least 18V, as otherwise, it could struggle to get through the wood.

3. Decoding Gardening Basics: The Ins and Outs of Gardening

Amending the Soil

As gardeners, our goal should be to keep our garden as healthy as can be so that it continues to produce fantastic results year after year. But doing this shouldn't mean spending a lot of money. A little bit of attention from time to time will allow you to keep the same soil in your raised garden bed for years without a problem? To look after our soil, we're going to amend it occasionally and make sure it is protected throughout the winter. By taking care of it before the start of winter and just after the end, you'll be able to keep your soil healthy for many seasons to come. You should still check on the quality of the soil when you can but this won't be necessary when the following steps are heeded.

When we mixed up our soil for our raised beds, we start from a base of 33% compost. This means that there are lots of nutrients in our garden soil to begin with. But as each harvest passes, there are going to be fewer and fewer nutrients in the soil. You should add compost either after you finish harvesting or in early spring when you start to prepare the beds. You will only need to do this once a year, otherwise, you could overload your soil. While this is one way to get lots of nutrients into the soil, we'll also be using a liquid fertilizer in a few moments and this will ensure that there are tons of nutrients available to the plants.

The organic elements in the soil will break down over time. When this happens, they start to stick together much tighter and the pathways through the soil start to get blocked up. This makes the soil tougher for roots to push through while also blocking access to oxygen and slowing down the drainage speed. As you water your garden throughout the first year, be mindful of how long it takes to dry out and the way the water soaks into it. When you first start, it will seem a little odd to be watching the water this closely but over time it will tell you about the quality of the soil. When it starts to slow down and really change, typically after 2 years or more, then you will know what is happening. At the beginning of the new growing season, you can either amend the soil by adding more sandy minerals to it or you can replace the soil with a fresh batch. It can be expensive to constantly replace the soil every few years. Amending is the much cheaper way to go but you need to be careful and take it slow. You could completely wreck the soil if you added too much of one thing in without mixing it around and getting a feeling for the texture.

Winter is a big change in the weather and you need to prepare your raised garden beds to weather the storms. First off, most gardeners yank their plants out at the end of the season so that they can replant in the following spring. This is a good idea but you should only cut away the above-soil part of the plant. Remove any root vegetables as well but you want to leave the roots. Over the course of the winter, they will turn into nutritious compost for your next crop. Speaking of compost, if you decide to add compost to the bed at the end of the growing season then you should make a layer of it on top, then cover this with a layer of mulch. This will make it so weeds can't get in, plus it will allow the compost to amend the soil and replenish many of the nutrients that were spent that summer.

If you aren't going to be mulching your raised garden beds then you should consider covering them using a strong plastic tarp. This will protect the soil and act in the place of mulch. It won't look quite as nice but if you are in an area where it snows a lot then you know that everything looks the same when it's buried in white fluff. It will be cheaper and far faster to put a tarp over your raised garden bed but mulching is the way to go if you are going to add compost before the winter. If you mulch, you can still use the tarp but it is rather redundant to use both methods.

By following these simple steps you can keep your soil lasting years. Checking on it throughout the season is important but making sure you prepare it for the winter and then "wake it up" again in the spring, it'll last you quite a while. The health of your soil is an investment well worth making. If you ignore it, you will find that it gets harder and harder to grow anything in your raised beds. You might think there is a problem with the bed while it is the soil at fault.

Water and Mulch Your Garden After Planting

After planting your crop, nourish it with adequate amounts of water. Make sure that the soil is only moistened, not drenched. You also need to mulch your garden with wood chips, leaves, straw, or grass clippings to keep the soil moist and prevent weeds.

Fertilizer for Your Garden

One of the best things you can do to feed your plants for your garden is not to pick the grass clippings. Let the clippings remain on the grass, instead of using a catcher on your mower. They'll decompose easily and bring essential nutrients back to your lawn. Fast, simple, and free-natural fertilization do not get much better.

Find seaweed, either gathered on its own or bought as a liquid extract from your garden center, for your vegetable and flower beds. This diamond is filled with minerals and trace elements; besides, if worked into the whole soil, its composition tends to help hold the plant's moisture. Most gardeners say this is the only fertilizer you'll ever have to use, and it's completely chemical-free.

When you have access to animal manure, consider using it; it's full of the nitrogen which your plants need. It's better to use rotted down manure, however, because fresh manure will burn the roots of your plants. All kinds of organic manure can be bought, from sheep and cows to the more exotic bat guano. Once it's worked into the soil, it's not nearly as smelly as you might think.

Many natural fertilizers that enjoy large use are blood and bone meal, beer (yep, beer), and coffee grounds.

Nonetheless, make sure that your soil is tested before adding something. You do not have to add something or add just 1-2 things, such as lime. You can't add anything. More is not better in fertilizer matters, and most plants can do well with a wise eye.

You will assist with the soil check and your local county extension office's definition so that you know exactly what you're dealing with. When you are dealing with your garden, it is always better to be safe than sorry!

Nutrient Requirements of Garden Plants

Plants mainly need macronutrients, i.e., nitrogen, phosphorus, and potassium:

- **Nitrogen (chemical symbol N).** It contributes to the development of foliage and stems or branches. It is an important fertilizer in the spring when the vegetation is recovering. But beware, used in excess, not only pollutes the water and the soil, but it unbalances the plants, which then produce more leaves at the expense of flowers and fruits. The most nitrogen-intensive plants are grass, grasses, bamboo, and leafy vegetables.

- **Phosphorus (chemical symbol P).** It contributes to the development of the roots, and it strengthens the resistance of plants in the face of diseases. Used in excess, it contributes to the eutrophication of water (that is to say, the proliferation of algae). The most demanding plants in phosphorus are flowering and fruiting species, as well as seed vegetables.

- **Potassium (chemical symbol K).** It contributes to flowering and fruit development. The most demanding plants in potassium are fruit trees, flowering shrubs, roses, bulbs, and root vegetables.

In variable proportions, the fertilizer can only have 1–2 elements or blends 3. Numbers showing the exact composition are accompanied by the initials of NPK. For example, a fertilizer containing 16% nitrogen (N), 5% phosphorus (P) and 5% potassium (K), will show "NKP 16-5-5."

Plants need secondary nutrients to a lesser extent such as calcium (C), sulfur (S), and magnesium (Mg), as well as trace elements

35

such as Iron (Fe), manganese (Mn), copper (Cu), zinc (Zn), silicon (Si), and more. But secondary nutrients are normally present in adequate amounts unless there is a soil deficiency or according to its PH. Your soil should be tested before any fertilizer supply to learn its strengths and imbalances.

Different Types of Fertilizers

Macronutrients, secondary nutrients, and trace elements come from different sources. Thus, nitrogen is present in dried blood, which is an organic fertilizer, and in nettle manure, which is considered an ecological fertilizer. Phosphorus comes from phosphate rock, so it is a mineral fertilizer, but it is also found in bone powder, which is an organic fertilizer. The same is true for potassium. Without forgetting that N, P, and K can also come from the chemical industry. It is, therefore, not by their composition that we can recognize this or that type of fertilizer but rather by their manufacture or their origin.

- **Chemical fertilizers.** These are synthetic products made from chemical elements.

- **Organic fertilizers.** They are of animal origin (powder bones or fish bones, dried blood, crushed horn, guano) or vegetable (algae, nettle manure or comfrey, ash, the residue of vinas, sugar, beet, etc.).

- **Mineral fertilizers.** They come from natural deposits of inert minerals such as potash or phosphate. But most of the time, they are actually made from chemical elements.

- **Ecological or natural fertilizers.** These are natural mineral fertilizers, organic fertilizers when they come from natural plant or animal materials. Nettle, comfrey purines are considered ecological fertilizers.

- **Green manures.** These are fast-growing plants (clover, alfalfa, lupine, horse bean, etc.), which are sown and buried on-site to provide a natural fertilizer rich in organic matter. In the garden, before installing a lawn, it is a good way to fertilize the soil.

Dealing With Pests and Diseases

The pests and diseases in the plants are not very different from the diseases and infections in human beings. The plants also get affected by pests and diseases in the same way, and if they aren't strong enough, the diseases and infections would win, leading to the destruction of your plants.

Human beings are more expressive, and hence, they can mostly cry out loud when they are affected by any problem. However, even in the case of human beings too, sometimes the diseases keep developing inside, and the parasites are also latent.

In the case of plants, finding out such problems can be very difficult, and you'll have to remain very vigilant to detect the problems developing in the plants or to stop a pest attack.

Big farmers engaged in commercial farming get affected by these issues, but they can deal with them with comparative ease due to their use of chemicals, pesticides, and insecticides. However, you may not want to take that route as this can contaminate the produce of the plants.

Consider These as Preemptive Actions

Location Is Important

Eskimos are believed to be very sturdy as they can survive in the coldest climate in the world. However, even for an Eskimo, surviving in the deserts of the Sahara may become an impossibility. You can't say that because even the African kids can survive in the Sahara, it should be easy for an Eskimo. The same is true for plants. The plants that need sunlight would develop diseases if they were kept in shade or humid environments. The chances of them developing mildew will remain exceptionally high. Therefore, it is very important that you identify the placement needs of the plants and do not compromise on that.

Develop an Understanding of Common Diseases and Pests

No matter how well you are prepared, there is always a possibility that the diseases widespread in the plants in that area might even affect your plants. The pests can travel, and they also get attracted by the conditions on-site, and hence, you must understand the common enemies so that you can take preventive steps in advance. If you know that diseases in the plants in your area are caused by a certain element, you can take preventive steps to avoid the development of such a situation. Keeping your eyes closed is not going to help at all. You must talk to the garden supplies seller in your area to have a clear understanding of the common diseases and pests so that your preparation can be better.

Plants With Better Immunity

It is a fact that not all the plants in a garden are affected by the same disease. If you know that a certain disease is more prevalent in your area, try to avoid having plants that are easily affected by that issue. There can be several other plants that wouldn't be getting affected by that disease, and you should go for them as this would help in reducing your headache a lot.

Provide Better Nutrition

This is another important factor that can help you in avoiding diseases. The plants that are strong and healthy have a better chance of being resistant to diseases. High-quality manure, balanced soil, and adequate water supply can help the plants in fighting diseases strongly.

Pests Like Easy Hiding Places

Once there is a pest infestation in your garden, getting rid of the pests can be a big challenge. The pests keep hiding from one place to another. However, this can be a bit difficult task in the beginning when the infestation has just begun as they are low in numbers and do not have proper hiding places. A clean garden would always make it difficult for the pests to hide. They would be easy to find and target. They'd also be easy prey for their predators. You must keep your garden clean and free of debris that provides shelter to the pests.

The Pests in the Garden

Birds

Birds are very common enemies of farmers. They can eat several fruits, vegetables, and grains. They can also be very helpful in eating several kinds of pests, but if you have grown something in the garden that interests you, then dealing with bird infestation can be a big challenge.

The best way to deal with this menace in raised bed gardens is to use any protective covering like a net that can prevent the access of birds. Raised bed structures are very helpful in holding the net coverings around the structure, and hence, that shouldn't prove to be a very difficult task to undertake.

This problem will only strike you if you have fruits and vegetables that interest them. If you only have decorative plants and flowers, there shouldn't be anything to worry about for you.

Slugs

These are the common enemies of young plants and seedlings. These are slow pests that may not look like a big threat, but if left ignored, they can cause havoc on your garden, especially the leafy plants. They munch on the plants endlessly, and they can destroy the seedlings completely.

The height of the bed is not just a problem for the slugs but also their predator hedgehogs. Even the hedgehogs would be unable to climb high-rise beds, and hence, the slugs that can climb the beds would be safe.

Carrot Flies

Carrots and parsnips are affected by these flies. These flies get attracted by the scent of the carrots and leave their maggot offspring on the vegetables. They can easily tunnel their way inside the roots. One option is to plant certain varieties that are resistant to these pests. Another option is to use very fine mesh shields around the plants to prevent these flies.

Cabbage Root Flies

As the name suggests, the flies affect the roots of the cabbage planted in the garden. The flies lay their eggs on the cabbage, and the larvae then make their way to the roots. Placing covering disks on top of the cabbage is a good solution to prevent flies from laying their eggs on the vegetable.

Aphids

These are the most common pests that feed on the plants. Easily infestation can be prevented by simply washing the plants with a soapy solution, but ladybugs can also be left in the garden to feed on these pests. Aphids can also become the meal of birds if you don't have fruits and vegetables in your garden that can be destroyed by the birds.

Mice and Rats

These can prove to be adamant pests, and if you have a mice infestation, dealing with it early on will be the best. Putting traps in place or keeping rat poisons in place are the most common solutions, but if the rat infestation is severe, you must consider taking the help of pest control agencies as it can also easily spread into your house. Rat and mice like to chew on newly planted seeds and plants, and they can also damage the produce.

The Diseases That Affect the Plants

Diseases can spread fast in the plants, and hence, it is always best to detect and deal with them early on. If you want to keep the diseases at bay, you must pay attention to your plant nutrition and hydration. Healthy plants are less likely to get affected by diseases easily.

Some of the common diseases are:

Botrytis

This is a fungal disease that affects soft fruits and vegetables. You'd notice a grey mold forming on the surface of the fruits like strawberries or vegetables like cabbage. This initial grey patch can lead to rot and decay of the whole fruit or vegetable. Poor ventilation in the area is the main cause of this mold development, and proper aeration on the raised bed can help in preventing the issue. If you notice this mold, remove the affected part to prevent further spread.

Powdery Mildew

This is another fungal infection that affects the leaves of the fruit trees like strawberries, gooseberries, and squash. The infection would cause the formation of white mildew on the leaves. A healthy and well-irrigated plant would be better suited to defend itself against this fungal infection. You can also get varieties that are resistant to this infection.

Club Root

This is yet another fungal infection that affects vegetables like cabbage and other root vegetables. Due to this infection, the root systems get swollen and distorted, leading to the death of the plant. Increasing alkalinity and crop rotation are some of the methods to prevent this infection.

Onion White Rot

This fungal infection can lead to browning and wilting of the foliage. If not addressed early on, it can finally lead to the rotting of the plant. Onion, leeks, and garlic are the common plant varieties that get affected by this fungal infection. If this fungus spreads to the raised bed, it can remain in the soil for years and keep affecting the plants again and again. Effective ways to deal with the issue are to either change the plant type or grow something different for a few seasons. You can also try changing the topsoil for a better and more effective solution to the problem.

Fertilizing Your Raised Bed Garden

When you start seedlings indoors, you begin to fertilize them. When seedlings start to sprout outdoors, you fertilize them. As your plants grow and mature, you fertilize them. It is only just before you harvest any edible vegetables that you stop fertilizing them because you don't want to add any more liquid to the soil. Fertilizing your plants is an absolute must if you want beautiful flowers or large yields.

Fertilizer comes in 2 types. There are fertilizers such as manure which can be added to and then mixed throughout the soil. A fertilizer like this is a good application at the start of spring or the end of fall. However, we can also mix in compost as a top layer with a blanket of mulch to protect our beds over the winter and add nutrients back into the soil. So, we're not going to worry about fertilizers that mix into the soil. Instead, we're going to stick with liquid fertilizer.

The other 3 important nutrients for us to worry about are nitrogen (N), phosphorus (P), and potassium (K). Together, these 3 nutrients play the biggest role in the development of your plant. Nitrogen is used to make the leaves of the plant grow faster and come in more fully. Phosphorus is used by the plants to strengthen the roots and make them grow big and strong. Potassium is a general nutrient that is used in multiple functions of the plant that are required for it to properly use and distribute energy from the sun and the soil. The 3 numbers on the soil refer to these 3 elements. This is the NPK ratio or the NPK balance and it tells you the percentage of nitrogen, phosphorus, and potassium in the fertilizer. It will always be in that order, NPK, so many labels don't bother labeling the numbers on the front.

Watering Your Raised Bed Garden

If you built your raised bed garden properly then watering it is going to be just as easy as watering any plants you grow outside. You are going to find that you need to water them a little bit more often than those in the ground but only by the slimmest of margins. Plants grown in containers tend to need to be watered more often and raised bed gardens are no different. But they're much larger and this slows down the process to the point where it won't be very noticeable. However, if you haven't properly built drainage holes into your raised garden bed frame then watering is going to make for a much more complicated experience. While raised beds do offer plants better protection from issues like root rot, a poor design can wipe that protection out and leave you with rotting plants.

Using the finger test will tell you if it is time to water them or not. You may quickly get into a rhythm of how often you need to water your raised beds, but you need to be careful not to get too confident if it is your first time gardening. The temperature is going to change throughout the growing period, and this is going to affect the rate of watering. Keep applying the finger test every day during your crop so that you understand what a garden bed goes through with the seasons and as the plants mature and come to harvest. The higher the temperature, the quicker the soil is going to dry out, and the more you will have to water your plants.

Maintenance Routine for Raised Bed Gardens

Raised bed gardening is an easy process. The initial setup process may look cumbersome; it makes the overall gardening experience smoother.

There are some simple things like keeping track of irrigation, timely weeding, taking care of the pests, and normal maintenance work, which may require your attention, or else, raised bed gardening doesn't keep you tied to a post. It is a very relaxed way to have the choicest plants in your garden.

The raised bed gardens are installed with 2 clear objectives:

- To increase the physical beauty of the landscape

- Help in growing useful plants

You can easily achieve both objectives with a little effort. Growing plants is comparatively easier, and the result is more promising than conventional gardening as the growing medium is very rich and raised bed gardening is easy.

There is no need to break your back by bending over for hours or doing constant tilling for aerating the land. Raised beds have an efficient water management system, and the soil is also prepared in a way that allows good aeration.

Irrigation, one of the biggest headaches in cultivation, can also be managed in a much better way in raised beds. The automation of the irrigation system is nothing new. There have been automatic irrigation systems in place for years, but in conventional gardening where the drainage system is not this efficient, even a little extra can cause waterlogging.

All these things get taken care of in raised bed gardening with greater ease. The whole system is overly advantageous for people who want to have beautiful gardens on their property but cannot devote a whole lot of time to the process. Raised bed gardening offers an easy way to manage your garden all year round.

Although raised bed gardening isn't very demanding and you are not required to be on your toes all year round. There are some simple management tasks that every gardener is supposed to do to ensure that the garden remains in the best of its shape.

Some simple gardening chores are required to be undertaken even in the winters when most plants are dormant or just waiting for the springs. You will have to devote some time even in this period to prepare the plants for the next season.

There are simple tasks like staking, pruning, deadheading, weeding, that need to be carried out all the time.

These tasks are important, and they help in making your garden beautiful and prepared for the next season.

Pruning, for example, is the simple task of chopping off the dead areas in the plants to stimulate growth in the next season. Most decorative plants need pruning, and it is an activity that can make your plant even better. However, pruning in the wrong season or the flowering season can be a big mistake because you'll be chopping off live buds. You'll have to do it in the winters when the plant isn't blooming but to prepare for the next season.

Some of the maintenance activities are:

Pruning

Pruning is the simple act of selectively removing unwanted branches to stimulate growth in the plant. A good prune helps in the removal of dead, broken, or damaged branches. If you don't prune on time, the branches from the trees or plants are going to fall anyway, but they are going to cause a mess and may even damage other plants. Pruning gives the tree a polished look and makes the overall landscape trimmer.

Most people don't pay attention to pruning. They either cut too deep or put a lot of stress on the plant as it will have to grow out from its lower seams. This should be avoided, and you must learn to prune at the right places.

Pruning at the right time is also equally important. You can start chopping off the branches and the buds in the wrong season. When the plants are about to bloom, there is no reason for you to chop off the tips. You might as well be chopping off the tips that were about to bloom. This is a task you'll need to undertake once the season is over, most probably in the winters.

Staking

Staking is another crucial activity that you'll need to undertake to make your garden look better. If you have ornamental plants to make your garden look beautiful, you will have to ensure that they remain in the right shape. You wouldn't want their branches to be falling over the edges or spread out onto the paths.

You must ensure that the plants are structured properly and take the right shape and form they are supposed to take.

Slings, nettings, supporting sticks, and teepees should be used properly to provide support to the growing plants to help them take the right shape.

Many people argue that plants should be allowed to grow naturally as they grow in the wild. It is not a very prudent thing to do in a garden where you only have a select number of plants, and space for them to grow is even more limited. Paying attention to staking is also a part of the crucial maintenance activity that you must undertake.

Maintenance and support activities are part and parcel of gardening work. There will be some activities that you will have to undertake even when it is the dormant season like the winters. This activity would help you in the blooming season.

4.   Life Begins With a Seed: How to Grow Plants From Seeds

Seeds vs. Seedlings

When it comes to planting your garden, you might wonder if it is better to plant the seed directly into the bed or plant a seedling instead. The answer to this question varies for different kinds of vegetables, but don't worry—by answering these 2 simple questions you will know what is the best choice for your favorite vegetable:

- **How long does the seed need to sprout?** Some plants take a long time to sprout and grow into seedlings. This means that if you live in a colder climate and the growing season is short, the plant might not have enough time to grow and mature if you plant the seeds in the bed at the beginning of the growing season. In that case, you can plant your seeds indoors a few weeks before the beginning of the growing season and transplant the seedlings into the beds once the weather is warmer.

- **Does the vegetable survive the transplant?** Some vegetables do well when transplanted, while others can't handle the shock. If a vegetable does not transplant well but takes a while to sprout, you can plant the seed directly into the raised beds, but create some kind of cover to protect the seedlings from frost. A milk carton or soda bottle with the bottoms cut out and placed over the plant works well for this.

Plants that you should direct seed: Beans, peas, radishes, carrots, parsnips, okra, garlic, lettuce, etc.

Plants that can be grown indoors for transplanting: Kale, broccoli, Brussels sprouts, endive, leeks, mustard greens, etc.

When to Plant Your Seeds/Seedlings

Not all vegetables should be planted at the same time of the year. Below I will give you a simple guide of the most common vegetables that you can grow in raised beds, along with the best time to start the seedlings and/or plant them into the beds. As the climates can greatly vary from one area to the other, I will give you a minimum temperature indication, that will ensure germination and prevent freezing. Check your region's last frost date and plan to plant your seeds/seedlings accordingly.

- **Tomatoes:** Plant seedlings when the temperature is a minimum of 55°F. Start seedlings indoors 6–8 weeks before the last spring frost.

- **Peppers:** Plant seedlings when the temperature is a minimum of 70°F. Start seedlings indoors 8–10 weeks before the last spring frost.

- **Lettuce:** Plant seedlings when the temperature is a minimum of 40°F. Start seedlings indoors 4–6 weeks before the last spring frost.

- **Broccoli:** Plant seedlings when the temperature is a minimum of 55°F. Start seedlings indoors 6–8 weeks before the last spring frost.

- **Cauliflower:** Plant seedlings when the temperature is a minimum of 65°F. Start seedlings indoors 6–8 weeks before the last spring frost.

- **Cabbage:** Plant seedlings when the temperature is a minimum of 40°F. Start seedlings indoors 6–8 weeks before the last spring frost.

- **Radishes:** Plant seeds in the bed when the temperature is a minimum of 39°F.

- **Peas:** Plant seeds in the bed when the temperature is a minimum of 34°F.

- **Beans:** Plant seeds in the bed when the temperature is a minimum of 48°F.

- **Carrots:** Plant seeds in the bed when the temperature is a minimum of 39°F.

- **Spinach:** Plant seeds in the bed when the temperature is a minimum of 55°F.

- **Radishes:** Plant seeds in the bed when the temperature is a minimum of 39°F.

Most vegetables that are planted as seeds directly into the ground need to be planted 1 week before to 1 week after the last spring frost. Make sure to check the package for more detailed instructions.

Tips for Ordering Vegetable Garden Seed

Thanks to the advent of the Internet, you can order seeds to plant in your vegetable without leaving the comfort of your home. When you are envisioning a beautiful and colorful vegetable garden in the next season, here are valuable tips that can help you to get your vegetable seed ordering together:

Make Sure That You Plan Your Vegetable Garden for the Entire Year

With the increasing popularity of backyard vegetable-raised gardening, a lot of gardeners are reporting the shortage of seeds. If you decide to wait until when it is summer in order to purchase seeds for fall planting, you may not be able to find the varieties that you need. Avoiding this kind of disappointment is easy, simply have a yearlong gardening plan and order seeds well ahead of your planting schedule.

Cover crops usually take up about one quarter (¼) of a garden's space all through the year—and do not fail to remember seeds for your winter gardening. In a milder climate, certain vegetables such as leeks, broccoli, garlic, and kale can grow all through the winter period without any protection. Then in early spring, these plants "take off" (start to grow), thus providing an early and a very much welcome spring harvest.

Access the Crops you Planted the Previous Year—in Order Conserve Your Efforts and Seed Money

Take a few moments in order to evaluate what you and your family enjoyed or totally disliked. Rather than grow huge peppers, you should consider planting quicker maturing small peppers; this way, you can enjoy the crops sooner. If your children totally ignored the green zucchini, then grow another plant, maybe a plant with bright yellow fruits.

You Can Achieve a Full-Size Harvest With Few Seeds

Do you know that the quantity of your harvest produce does not usually connect with the number of plants in the ground? You can save some seeds by simply growing a smaller number of plants but providing them with a favorable growing environment. By simply spacing your plants further apart, and providing them with an equal amount of nutrients as the large plants, every plant will become much more productive.

Preserve Your Seed Investments by Properly Storing and Labeling

When you get your seeds by mail, make sure that you label each seed packet with the present date—many gardeners overlook this important part. Store the seed packets in a re-sealable plastic bag or air-tight containers in order to ensure that the seeds stay dry. For additional protection, you can add desiccant packs in order to absorb any moisture within the storage area.

You should store the seeds in a dry, dark, and cool location (not in the freezer!) You should store the seeds in a temperature range of 40–50°F (4–10°C). Correct seed storage is a vital factor for reliable seed germination.

Be Organized

You may lose or waste lots of vegetable garden seeds simply by being disorganized. So, ensure that you keep a folder for your garden where you keep your seed order duplicates, garden charts, plant tags, and planting information. It is highly recommended that you keep a notebook or use garden maps where you will be able to document when you plant, what the climatic conditions were, and how your plants thrived. After you visit other veterans' raised gardens, write down their advice and gardening observation. Most times, we often remember the gardening tips and ideas that we have learned from friends, but if you do not write them down in your gardening folder, you may end up forgetting these gardening ideas. In addition to this, one day in the future, your kids may find a 40-year-old gardening journal that they may find really useful.

Growing a vegetable garden is really rewarding on so many levels; however, it all starts with a seed. Learning from your own experience and the advice gotten from veteran gardeners will help you get the most out of every penny of your seed-buying dollar and assist you to realize your vision of a beautiful and colorful vegetable garden.

5. It's All Part of the Plan: Successful Gardeners Follow a Plan

Spacing Between Plants

You can adhere to the typical garden plant spacing, which is in rows, or you might choose the square foot gardening that helps you use most of your space. This is done by marking off the garden bed in 12-inch square sections. Then you can start planting your seeds, one type of plant for each square. You can make a personalized diagram of your beds, so you know which plants you have planted in every square.

Block planting is also recommended with proper spacing between plants to achieve better plant production. For large plants like tomatoes or squash, you will have to make 24-inch centers. If you are trying to grow medium-sized crops like peas, onions, and beans, you'll need to plant them 4–6-inch apart. If your garden is for small crops like root crops and green leafy vegetables, you'll simply need to scatter the seeds over a small section of your garden's soil.

Position Plants Strategically

It is recommended that you put plants that need less care in the middle part of the bed and those that require more care on the edges. If only one side of your raised bed garden can be reached by sunlight, you need to do 2 things—Place the smaller ones toward the southern part and the taller plants on the northern part. If you are planting cucumbers, position them near the edge of the bed to allow them to trail over the side.

Determine the Right Depth

It is necessary to determine the right depth for the crop that you are trying to grow. To begin, you have to know that a minimum of 6-inch deep is necessary for most vegetables to grow well above ground. For root vegetables, a depth of 10–12-inch is necessary. However, some crops don't need to be covered with thick soil. If you are planting lettuce, you need to make a ½-inch deep furrow before sprinkling the seeds into every hole. You may then sprinkle a thin layer of soil to cover the lettuce seeds. If you are planting carrots, cover the seeds with fine-textured potting soil.

Interplanting

If you know how to plant a raised garden with plants that prefer different moisture levels, you know that the key is interplanting. Interplanting is mixing several different types of plants in one bed.

Tips on interplanting:

- You should plant melons under pea plants. This way they don't crowd each other out.

- You shouldn't plant borage and asparagus in the same bed. Asparagus loves to drink water and the borage will wilt if there is too much water in the soil.

- You should not plant carrots and endive together if you plan to use compost containing peat moss. You will want to plant the endive when you harvest the carrots.

- You shouldn't place a plant that matures quickly with one that takes its time to grow and ripen. You don't want to be harvesting and disturb the ones that aren't ready, right?

Practice Companion Planting

Just like other gardening methods, you can also take advantage of companion planting to reduce the risk of pest infestation. Allow compatible plants to grow close together and benefit from one another. You can plant beans with corn to increase nitrogen supply or with borage to repel worms in tomatoes. You can also grow peppers with spinach in between. This will allow the peppers to provide shade to the spinach and extend its picking season to make it more delicious.

However, you need to remember that there are crop combinations you need to avoid, such as corn and tomatoes. These crops attract the same pest, such as corn earworms or tomato fruit worms.

Succession Planting

As much as you might want to reap lots of goodies, keep in mind that too much of something is not good. When you plant all the seeds in the package at once will result in a glut of produce. That's why you need to practice succession planting.

Avoid planting all the seeds at once and instead sow only a quarter of the seeds after every 2 weeks to avoid feast or famine.

Also, plant a quick maturing plant such as spinach and once you harvest that crop, replace it with another plant such as lettuce. Once you gather the lettuce, plant tomatoes, peppers, or another heat-loving crop.

Crop Rotation

It is extremely important that you practice crop rotation in your raised beds to prevent the build-up of pests and diseases in the soil. As you are using raised beds these are going to be low initially, but if you grow the same crop year after year in the same bed then you will encounter problems as the pests or diseases targeting that particular crop build up.

Crop rotation is key to successfully growing vegetables because not only does it reduce pests and diseases, but it helps to ensure that the soil retains vital nutrients and micro-organisms which are beneficial to your plants. Add in succession planting and you further help the soil whilst getting even more out of your vegetable plot!

Crop rotation is perfectly natural, having been practiced by farmers for thousands of years as it is vital to maintain soil quality and interrupt the lifecycle of pests. However, remember that this only applies to annual plants and not your perennial plants such as asparagus, fruit bushes, and so on. These stay in the same place year after year, but you will have to work the soil and many people move them when they have outlived their usefulness or reached the end of their life. Applying manure or fertilizer once or twice during a growing season is often enough to keep these permanent plants happy.

Crop rotation helps to reduce the severity and incidences of diseases such as tomato or potato blight, onion/leek rust, and many others, as well as crop-specific pests. As you do not grow the same crop in the same soil season after season, the diseases do not have the opportunity to build up. Some pests or diseases will live in the soil for a few years and by rotating your crop you ensure these pests die out before they have a chance to establish themselves.

To make the most out of crop rotation:

- Plant legumes such as beans then follow them up with heavy feeders; for example, plant beans one year, then the next year plant tomatoes.

- Alternate deep-rooted crops with shallow-rooted crops such as beets the first year and follow with cauliflower next.

- Maximize space and increase yield by growing long seasoned crops with short-season crops in the same bed.

Those are the 3 main practices you need to keep in mind to increase your success in vegetable farming. Now, next are some proven tips to supplement these practices and guidelines for growing each crop.

Greenhouse

Greenhouse gardening can then be defined as the science of growing plants in an erected building with materials usually transparent or translucent such that the plants are provided with controlled favorable environmental conditions. Plants that are cultivated in greenhouses receive protection against conditions like soil erosion, harsh weather, violent rain and storm, plant pathogens, etc. This system of gardening is also called glasshouse or hothouse by some growers, and the major reason for setting it up is arguably so as to secure a considerable quantity of water vapor and heat in order to maintain humidity and proper temperature in the greenhouse.

A greenhouse is designed to keep heat inside the building. It allows sunlight to enter and warm the inside of the building. The structure is insulated, which prevents heat from escaping.

Most parts of the greenhouse are made from clear plastic or glass because these materials allow more natural sunlight to pass through. Sunlight is the main source of thermal energy, as well as a crucial source of energy for plant photosynthesis. In addition, it warms up the ground and the air inside the greenhouse. The sun-warmed ground provides additional heating long after the sun goes down. The insulation system keeps this heat within the structure to maintain the desired temperatures.

Purposes of a Greenhouse

Modern uses of greenhouses include shielding plants from the extremes of temperatures that may damage them. It makes it possible to grow plants during the cold months to sustain a steady supply of fresh food. Seasonal fruits can be enjoyed year-round. A greenhouse can be made to simulate the growing conditions of a particular fruit, even if the outside weather is totally different. Summer fruits can be enjoyed in the winter. Tropical fruits can be served in the homes of those in the Northern hemisphere.

Greenhouse gardening extends the growing season of valuable crops like tomatoes and corn. The controlled environment allows for better crop yield. Changing weather can often devastate crops, but not so if grown within a greenhouse. Flowers can be grown all year-round, too. Horticulture fans and flower lovers can cultivate flowers that do not grow naturally in their areas. Cold northern places can very well grow tropical flowers within greenhouses. Rare orchids can be cultivated in colder areas. All these thanks to greenhouses.

Extending Your Growing Season

Raised beds allow you to extend your growing season because they are naturally warmer than the surrounding soil. However, you can also easily turn your raised bed into a cold frame or cover it with fleece using some of the techniques. This allows you to extend your growing season and get even more out of your raised beds.

Of course, the same techniques can be used to start your plants off earlier on! If you cover your soil with black plastic sheeting around 6–8 weeks before the last frost date it will heat the soil. You then cover the soil with a clear plastic tunnel and when the soil hits 65–70°F you cover the black plastic with straw and put your plants in place. The straw stops the plastic from heating too much whilst the plastic retains moisture and heat. When the weather has warmed sufficiently you remove the plastic tunnel.

Your Garden Knowledge

In addition to choosing the style for your garden, you have to understand all the various climatic and geological factors that characterize the area you are planning. It is essential to understand the climate, how often it rains, how much wind is there, how many hours of sunlight illuminate the area for example.

Once you have an answer to these questions surely you will be able to choose which plants, flowers, and shrubs are best suited.

The healthiest gardens include interactions with the native environment and it is important to use plants that will naturally thrive there.

Consider a part of your garden. Is your garden facing south? North? East? West? Understanding the direction will allow you to find out where you want everything to go.

When planning your landscape, think about your local climate, the topography of your site, and your type of soil. The use of the "USDA Plant Hardiness Zone Map" is a great starting point.

Gardening Through the Seasons

Cool-Season Crops

Do best when the temperature is about 55–70°F—beets, broccoli, brussels sprouts, collards, garlic, leeks, lettuce, mustard, onions, parsnips, peas, radishes, rutabaga, shallots, spinach, Swiss chard, turnips.

Warm-Season Crops

Do best when the temperature is about 65–80°F—beans, snap, lima, beans, shell (dry), corn, cucumber, eggplant, melons, New Zealand spinach, okra, peppers, potatoes, pumpkins, squash, summer squash, sunflowers, sweet potatoes, tomatillos, tomatoes, watermelons, zucchini.

Climate and Vegetables

The following chart will help you determine when to plant each crop directly in the garden this spring. It uses the middle of each month as a marker. If the date of your average last frost varies by 1–2 weeks in either direction, then simply adjust the planting dates by 1–2 weeks.

When to Plant

Vegetables	If the last frost in spring Feb. 15	If the last frost in spring Feb. 15	If the last frost in spring April 15	If the last frost in spring May 15
Arugula	Feb. 1–Mar. 1	Mar. 1–15	Apr. 1–May 1	May 15–June 1
Asparagus	––	Feb. 1–Mar. 10	Apr. 15–May 1	May 15–June 1
Asian greens	Feb. 1–Mar. 1	Mar. 1–15	Apr. 1–May 1	May 15–June 1
Beans—lima	Mar. 1–May. 1	Apr. 1–15	May 15–June 1	May 15–June 15
Beans—snap	Mar. 1–May 1	Mar. 15–30	May 1–June 1	May 15–June 1
Beet	Jan. 20–Apr. 1	Mar. 1–15	Apr. 15–May 1	May 15–June 1
Broccoli	Jan. 15–Feb. 15	Feb. 15–Mar. 1	Mar. 15–Apr. 15	May 1–15
Brussels sprouts	Jan. 15–Feb. 15	Feb. 15–Mar. 1	Mar. 15–Apr. 15	May 1–15
Cardoon	Jan. 1–Feb. 1	Feb. 15–Mar. 1	Mar. 15–Apr. 15	May 1–15
Chives	Jan. 1–Feb. 1	Feb. 15–Mar. 1	Mar. 15–Apr. 15	May 1–15

Claytonia	Jan. 1–Feb. 25	Feb. 15–Mar. 1	Mar. 15–Apr. 15	May 1–15
Corn	Feb. 15–Mar. 1	Mar. 15–Apr. 1	Apr. 15–May 15	May 15–June 15
Cress	Feb. 1–Mar. 1	Mar. 1–15	Apr. 1–May 1	May 15–June 1
Cucumber	Mar. 1–15	Apr. 1–15	May 1–June1	May 15–June 1
Dandelion	Jan. 1–Feb. 1	Feb. 1–Mar. 15	--	--
Eggplant plants	Mar. 1–15	Apr. 1–15	May 1–June 1	June 1–15
Florence fennel	Feb. 1–Mar. 1	Mar. 1–15	Apr. 1–May 1	May 15–June
Garlic	Jan. 1–Feb. 1	Feb. 15–Mar. 1	Mar. 15–Apr. 15	May 1–15
Horseradish	--	Mar. 15–Apr. 1	Apr. 15–May 1	May 15–June 1
Jerusalem artichoke	Jan. 1–Feb. 1	Feb. 15–Mar. 1	Mar. 15–Apr. 15	May 1–June 1
Leek	Jan. 1–Feb. 1	Feb. 15–Mar. 1	Mar. 15–Apr. 15	01/05/01
Lettuce	Feb. 1–Mar. 1	Mar. 1–15	Apr. 1–May 1	May 15–June1

Mâché	Feb. 1–Mar. 1	Mar. 1–15	Apr. 1–May 1	May 15–June 1
Muskmelon	Mar. 1–15	Apr. 1–15	May 1–June 1	01/06/15
Mustard	Feb. 1–Mar. 1	Mar. 1–15	Apr. 1–May 1	May 15–June 1
Okra	Feb. 1–Mar. 1	Mar. 15–30	May 1–15	--
Onion plants	Jan. 1–Feb. 1	Feb. 15–Mar. 1	Mar. 15–Apr. 15	May 1–15
Onion seeds	Feb. 1–Mar. 1	Mar. 1–15	Apr. 1–May 1	May 15–June1
Onion sets	Jan. 1–Feb. 1	Feb. 15–Mar. 1	Mar. 15–Apr. 15	May 1–15
Parsley	Feb. 1–Mar. 1	Mar. 1–15	Apr. 1–May 1	May 15–June 1
Parsnip	Feb. 1–Mar. 1	Mar. 1–15	Apr. 1–May 1	May 15–June 1
Peas	Jan. 1–Feb. 1	Feb. 15–Mar. 1	Mar. 15–Apr. 15	May 1–June 1
Pepper plants	Mar. 1–15	Apr. 1–15	May 1–June 1	--
Potato	Jan. 1–Feb. 1	Feb. 15–Mar. 1	May 1–June 1	May 1–June

Pumpkin	Mar. 1–15	Apr. 1–15	May 1–June 1	--
Radish	Jan. 1–Feb. 1	Feb. 15–Mar. 1	Mar. 15–Apr. 15	
Rhubarb plants	--	--	Apr. 1–May 1	May 1–June 1
Rutabaga	Mar. 1–Mar. 15	Apr. 1–15	May 1–June 1	June 1–15
Salsify	Feb. 1–Mar. 1	Mar. 1–15	Apr. 15–May 1	May 1–June 1
Scallions	Jan. 1–Feb. 1	Feb. 15–Mar. 1	Mar. 15–Apr. 15	01/05/01
Shallots	Jan. 1–Feb. 1	Feb. 15–Mar. 1	Mar. 15–Apr. 15	May 1–15
Sorrel	Jan. 1–Feb. 1	Mar. 1–Apr. 1	Apr. 1–15	May 1–15
Spinach	Feb. 1–Mar. 1	Mar. 1–15	Mar. 15–Apr. 15	May 1–15
Squashes	Mar. 1–15	Apr. 1–15	May 1–June 1	June 1–15
Sweet potato	Mar. 1–15	Apr. 1–15	May 1–June 1	--
Swiss chard	Jan. 1–Feb. 1	Feb. 15–Mar. 1	Mar. 15–Apr. 15	May 1–15

Tomatillo plants	Mar. 1–15	Apr. 1–15	May 1– June 1	––
Tomato plants	Mar. 1–15	Apr. 1–15	May 1– June 1	June 15–30
Turnips	Mar. 1–15	Apr. 1–15	May 1– June 1	June 1–15
Watermelon	Mar. 1–15	Apr. 1–15	May 1– June 1	01/06/00

Vegetable for Beginners

Beets, beans, broccoli, Brussels sprouts, cabbage, carrots, collards, corn, cucumbers, kale, kohlrabi, lettuce, onions, melons, peas, peppers, potatoes, pumpkins, rutabagas, summer squash, tomatoes, turnips.

Vegetables to Plant in Summer

Tomatoes, okra, peppers, amaranth, squash, beans, greens, berries, sweet potatoes, southern peas, cucumbers, Manoa lettuce, eggplant, sorrels, melons, Malabar spinach, corn, shallots.

Vegetables to Plant in Spring

Radishes, spinach, mesclun greens, lettuce, Swiss chard, spring greens, mustard greens, turnips, broccoli, cauliflower, carrots, potatoes, peas, mache, gai lan or choi sum, bok choy, onions.

Vegetables to Plant in Autumn

Snow peas, baby spinach, bok choy, radish, kale, garlic, beetroot, broccoli, lettuce, carrots, Asian salad greens, silverbeet, coriander, onion, strawberries, lemon.

Maintenance Activities for Every Season of the Year

Winter

- **Raised bed repairing and maintenance work:** Winters are the best time to carry out all the maintenance and repair work on the raised beds as several plants wouldn't be there. There will not be plants in bloom, and hence, there is no fear of plants getting hurt. It is the dormant season, and you can easily undertake the repair work. You must carefully inspect the structure of the raised beds as a wooden structure can start rotting, and even brick structures develop holes and gaps. It is the best time of the year to carry out the mending work.

- **New construction:** This time of the year, when another gardening activity is low, you can also devote time to the construction of new raised beds, building paths, and doing other such works that may make it easier for you to grow more in the next season. Devote time to create compost as it can be used as fertilizer in the coming months. This time can be used for fermentation.

- **Soil improvement:** Soil improvement is a continuous activity that you need to carry out. This time of the year when there are very few plants on the raised bed, you get a good chance to add manure to the soil and improve its quality. In this process, you also upturn the soil, and hence, the buildup of pests and diseases can also be prevented in this way.

- **Stock up for the next growing season:** This is the correct time to think of the things you'd like to plant in the next growing season. You can start buying the seeds for planting in the spring and summer.

- **Prune:** This is a good time to prune the flowers, ornamental trees, fruit trees, and shrubs. This is the time when pruning helps the most as there is no damage to chopping off the buds, and the trees get a good amount of time to have growth.

- **Plant new trees and shrubs:** This is also a good time to plant new ornamental trees and shrubs.

Spring

- **Mulching:** It is a crucial activity that can help a lot. Mulching in the springtime helps in retaining the moisture well and leads to the suppression of weeds that are desperately trying to make their way in this season. You must do mulching early in the springs.

- **Staking:** This is another important activity that you must undertake in the spring. Putting climbing structures in place early on is very helpful for several plants.

- **Watch out for the pests:** This is the time when the development of diseases and pests begins. If you remain watchful in the springtime, you will be able to prevent the spread of diseases and pests much before there is an outbreak in your garden.

Summer

- **Deadheading:** You know the role deadheading plays in the growth of plants, and this is the correct time to deadhead the plants. This will ensure that they keep flowering the whole season.

- **Extending the season:** Early summer is the best time to cut the herbaceous perennial plants to the ground level so that they can flower up from there. If you do it in early summer, you will have a chance to extend the season. They'd start flowering at a lower level and remain contained.

- **Weeding season:** This is also the right time to weed out. Both perennial and annual weeds spring up around this time. You'll have ample sun to dig out the weeds from their roots and expose them to the sun. Careful weeding this season can help you in saving a lot of headaches later.

- **Focus on plant hydration:** Watering the plants around this time is very important as evaporation increases in this season. It may be the correct time to recalibrate your irrigation system to cater to the increased needs of the plants.

Autumn

- **Planting time:** This is the good time of the year when the soil is still warm and protective for the seeds to grow. You should carry out all the planting activities this season. The warmth in the soil would give the plants a better chance to expand and strengthen their position in the soil. Planting early in the autumn would prepare the plants better to fight off the winters.

- **Composting:** This is the time a lot of green material falls off the ground. You must gather all of it and use it for composting that could be used in the spring.

6. Grow Your Garden to Success: How to Grow Vegetables, Herbs, Fruit, and Cut Flowers

Best Veggies to Grow in Raised Garden Beds

A vegetable nursery is certifiably not a low maintenance space, however, with a touch of arranging, soil care, great site determination, and savvy crop decisions, it can absolutely turn into a low maintenance garden. In case if you're new to cultivating or only close on schedule, keep it basic and keep it little. You may grow a ton of food in a solitary raised bed or a couple of holders. Furthermore, on account of persevering plant raisers, we have such a significant number of conservative vegetable assortments to browse.

Just before you kick things off in another nursery, glance around. Your picked site should offer a lot of daylight, in any event, 8 hours of each day. Most vegetables don't value having wet feet, so very much depleted soil is likewise significant. If your current soil is not exactly perfect, a raised bed might be your best alternative. Raised beds offer such huge numbers of points of interest. They warm up from the get-go in spring, channel well, and can be seriously planted, which implies more food in less space. It additionally pays to pull weeds off before they blossom and set seeds. In case you're prepared to be a raised bed cultivator, you'll discover a lot of new information below regarding vegetable planting.

Best Soil for Veggies to Grow

Focus on your soil structure; sound soil is everything you may need to plant in the right way. These might be the absolute most effortless vegetables to develop, yet they're not going to be cheerfully planted in poor soil. Dive in some fertilizer or matured compost before planting and again between progressive yields to keep your yield increasing. Cultivating in a raised bed, you need to utilize a top-notch preparing blend, not garden soil, mixed with fertilizer for your pruned vegetables. Likewise, it is preferred to include granular natural vegetable food in your raised beds and compartment gardens at planting time to take care of plants throughout the entire season.

At last, in case you're still wavering about structure or making another nursery bed only for vegetables, consider that a considerable lot of these harvests like beans, cherry tomatoes, and garlic can be planted in existing bloom gardens. It is often said that vegetables and blossoms make flawless plant buddies.

Easiest Vegetables to Grow in a Raised Bed Garden

- **Beans.** Shrubbery beans are practically secure as they go from seed to gather in less than 2 months and offer a long time of delicate harvest. Beans acknowledge warm soil and warm climate, so don't surge spring planting. Plant seeds after the last snow, planting them 2-inch separated in lines that are dispersed around for 18-inch separately. When the seedlings are developing great, move the shrub beans bushes to 6-inch. Plant a rainbow of beans; grow a blend of green, purple, yellow, and even red assortments.

- **Green peas.** Peas possess a flavor like spring. There are a couple of various kinds of peas: snow peas, sugar snap, and shell peas, and all are anything but difficult to develop. Sow in the pea seeds in late winter when you can relax and let the soil settle, around 4 weeks to about 1 ½ month before the last anticipated snow. Sow in the seeds 1–2-inch separated in twofold lines separated by 6-inch. If you're growing an assortment that should be marked, it's a smart thought to include a pea trellis or drape netting before you plant. Peas can likewise be developed in holders also.

- **Tomatoes.** Cherry tomatoes are the main nursery vegetable developed in North America. Huge fruited assortments set aside an extended effort to convey their harvest, yet fast-developing cherry tomatoes begin delivering around 2 months from transplanting. Start with solid seedlings from the nursery community, planting them in garden beds or enormous compartments once the danger of spring snow has passed.

In the nursery, stick to early developing, profitable cherry tomatoes like Sun Gold (insane sweet), Jasper (curse safe), or Sunrise Bumble Bee. These will require a tough stake or backing embedded at planting time. Bind the plant to the stake with twine as it develops.

- **Squash.** It's a nursery plant regardless of what number of summer squash plants you develop. You will consistently have beyond what you can eat and irrespective of whether you just planted one. Directly sow the seeds in the bed very much altered with fertilizer or compost after the previous spring. When natural products start to shape, harvest regularly with time for top quality and flavor. For patty pan and round assortments, pick when the natural products are a few inches in breadth. Pick zucchini when they're 4–6-inch in length. There are a ton of lovely assortments to attempt in your nursery.

- **Cucumbers.** The invigorating mash of a just-picked garden cucumber is one of the preferred approaches to chill off on a blistering summer day. Cucumbers are warm-season veggies. Directly seed them in garden beds or holders 7 days after the previous spring snow or, on the other hand, spare time and plant seedlings bought from a nearby nursery community. Give them a lot of fertilizer and water reliably for the most excellent cucumbers. In the event that space is short, take a stab at developing smaller hedge cucumbers.

- **Garlic.** Garlic is the easiest growing vegetable. Take care of individual cloves in mid-harvest time in the nursery. Try not to harvest until the next year in right on time to mid-summer. The plants are irritated by not many pests or maladies and develop fine in ordinary nursery soil. Try not to plant general store garlic. Rather, purchase garlic for planting from your nearby nursery community. When planted, mulching the beds with straw can hold soil dampness and decrease the weeds. Collect when half of the leaves have changed their color, draping the plants to fix in a dry spot for about 14 days. In the wake of restoring, cleaning, and storing bulbs, it truly is probably the most effortless vegetable to develop.

- **Lettuce.** While most servings of mixed greens are quick to go from seed to gathering it, leaf lettuce is the simplest and quickest of them all. Sow in the seeds legitimately in the garden beds in mid-spring sprinkling them in a 6-inch wide band. Keep the seedbed equitably soggy until the plants are developed admirably. You can grow leaf lettuce in holders, window boxes, and textured developed sacks. They are prepared to pick when they're 2–4-inch in length. If you cut leaves from the outside of the plant, the inside will keep on developing, dragging out the harvesting season.

- **Bell peppers.** Peppers require a breeze to develop. Essentially, you plant them and watch them take off. However, for most extreme production, a bit of pampering makes a difference. Grow the peppers in a bed that gets full sun. Give sandy topsoil that channels well and contains a lot of natural organic matter. Most sweet peppers develop in 60–90 days; hot peppers can take as long as 150–180 days. Remember, in any case, that the quantity of days to development expressed on the seed parcel refers to the days in the wake of transplanting until the plant creates a full-sized organic product.

Growing Chart

Crop	Number of days for germination	Number of weeks to optimum age for transplanting	Amount of light* required	Number of days from seeding to harvest
Beans	5-8	-	Sun	45-65
Cucumbers	6-8	3-4	Sun	50-70
Eggplant	8-12	6-8	Sun	90-120
Lettuce, leaf	6-8	3-4	Partial Shade	45-60
Onions	6-8	6-8	Partial Shade	80-100
Parsley	10-12	-	Partial Shade	70-90
Pepper	10-14	6-8	Sun	90-120
Radish	4-6	-	Partial Shade	20-60
Squash	5-7	3-4	Sun	50-70
Tomato	7-10	5-6	Sun	90-130

Best Herbs to Grow in Raised Garden Beds

There are numerous advantages to developing herbs in your raised beds. Various herbs have diverse dampness needs, and developing them in pots is a simple method to control soil dampness. Obviously, developing herbs in holders will likewise keep forceful spreaders, similar to mint, leveled out and away from garden beds. Following are some herbs that are very easy and best to grow in a raised bed garden:

- **Basil.** Basil is a hot climate herb grown annually and thrives when grown in compartments and raised beds. Several nursery workers battle to grow fresh basil, yet give it all-around soil and 6 hours of sunshine, and it's generally great going. Similar to many herbs, basil will keep on developing even when cut off. There is no uncertainty; it's probably the easiest herb for raised bed cultivating. Likewise, keep in mind to remove any flower buds that sprout. When basil starts to bloom, the leaf flavor decays.

- **Oregano leaves.** This could be an excellent product in the garden, and keeping it in a bed is an excellent and straightforward approach to managing its growth. The small leaves are filled with flavor, perfect for fixing custom-made pizza, just as adding to pasta and other Italian dishes. Greek oregano gives the most exotic flavor for cooking use.

- **Rosemary.** This is a woody shrub with sweet-smelling, needle-like foliage that adds an inviting depth of flavor to cooked potatoes and chicken dishes. Rosemary is a yearly herb; however, developing it in raised beds makes it simple to plant. The fastest approach to execute compartment-developed rosemary is by watering it to an extreme; it needs high dampness.

- **Thyme.** Thyme is perhaps the best herb for raised bed planting; it needs very low maintenance; it is a dry season plant and can take a touch of less care. Besides, it looks incredible when planted at the front of a compartment where the leaves can hill over the edge of the raised bed. Give it full sun and don't overwater; it's dry, spell-safe, and lean towards its soil on the dry side.

- **Mint.** Mint is a very easy-growing herb in a raised bed garden. It immediately dominates despite everything hauling it out. Presently, developing mint in pots is preferred. Utilizing a 66% fertilized soil to 33% fertilizer blend in your mint-raised beds is recommended. There are such a huge number of wonderful sorts of mint— peppermint, chocolate mint, mojito mint, strawberry mint, and spearmint, for instance. We add the leaves to summer drinks, a plate of mixed greens, and furthermore dry bounty for winter tea. Mint acknowledges adequate dampness and rich soil.

- **Parsley.** Basil might be a main culinary herb, yet parsley is nearby a second. The extraordinary leaf surface of wavy parsley makes it a decent planting accomplice for fancy plants like million chimes, geraniums, petunias, and other summer shorts. Parsley is extremely simple to develop, however, like mint, wants more dampness and good care. It is recommended to use natural compost at planting time to keep the plants secure from spring through late harvest time. Parsley likewise acknowledges full sun; however, it can take some light concealing.

- **Cilantro.** It appears to be everybody's favorite and everyone has a solid assessment about the flavor of this herb it is possible that you love it or detest it. Regardless of whether you appreciate eating cilantro, it can at present be a helpful herb in the nursery. When on the grounds, its solid fragrance will really repulse pests.

Some Tricks for Growing Herbs in Raised Beds

- Usual harvesting with pruners or herb cuts energizes new development, so don't be bashful about squeezing and cutting your homegrown herbs.

90

- It can be fun to fill your compartments with garden soil. However, garden soil rapidly compacts in pots, decreasing soil seepage and sponginess. Fill your pots with fertilized soil or a mix of gardening soil and mature manure. Worm castings are likewise a simple way to help your soil supplemented and moisture maintained, and you just require to add a bunch to the beds also.

- In case you're new to herb cultivating, consider doing a little dig out regarding different herbs. Certain herbs favor all around depleted soil (rosemary, thyme, and oregano), while others like more dampness (mint, parsley, and coriander).

- To increase sound development, feed your herbs with compost that is reasonable for edibles.

Growing Chart

Type of herb	Indoor seed starting or direct sow	When to start indoors (weeks before last expected spring frost)	When to direct sow	Planting depth
Basil	Indoor	6 to 8 weeks		1/4 inch deep
Common Chamomile	Both	6 weeks	After last frost	On soil surface
Chives	Indoor	10 to 12 weeks		1/4 inch deep
Cilantro	Direct sow		1 to 2 weeks before last frost	1/2 inch deep
Dill	Both	6 weeks	After last frost	1/4 inch deep
Lavender	Indoor	10 to 12 weeks		1/8 inch deep
Lemon Balm	Indoor	6 to 8 weeks		1/8 inch deep
Mint	Indoor	10 weeks		1/4 inch deep
Oregano	Indoor	10 to 12 weeks		On soil surface
Parsley	Indoor	10 weeks		1/4 inch deep
Rosemary	Indoor	10 to 12 weeks		
Summer Savory	Both	6 to 8 weeks	After last frost	1/4 inch deep
Thyme	Indoor	14 to 16 weeks		On soil surface

Best Fruits to Grow in Raised Garden Beds

Who would not love to fetch a new, delicious peach or a bunch of strawberries from their own grown garden? There are numerous organic products you can develop in your home nursery, regardless of whether you have a restricted space. Yet, before you plant, put some idea into which organic products develop best in your atmosphere, according to the arrangement of your nursery. Organic product trees and bushes can live for a long time and require appropriate daylight, soil, and air course.

Regardless of the fact that your organic product assortment is strong, subzero and drying winds can slaughter the delicate buds, bringing about no natural product for the season. The equivalent can happen when pre-summer ice hits the buds. You can't control the climate, yet planting in a shielded area, for example, close to a fence or support, will help. At the point when you develop your own products of the soil, you will get all the fun of planting in addition to the farm to fork goodness and sustenance that alone accompanies homegrown harvests. The accompanying and simple to develop edibles show exactly how basic developing and making the most of your own foods grown from the ground can be. The following are the best fruits to grow in your raised bed garden:

- **Blueberries.** Berries are a simple fruit to try at developing an organic product. Blueberries contain 3-season bushes with pretty white spring blossoms, summer natural products, and ravishing red fall foliage. Developing blueberries requires some development work to guarantee the soil surface is sufficiently fermented. However, the bushes should live and create a natural product for a considerable length of time. For an enormous harvest, you will require 2 assortments for good fertilization.

  You can likewise develop blueberries in holders. Simply keep in mind to cover your plants with mesh to shield them from flying creatures once the natural product shows up.

- **Strawberries.** Newly picked strawberries are certainly justified regardless of the insignificant stress it takes to develop them. You may have a decision among 3 kinds: June bearing, which sets one huge yield in June (decent for jam making and freezing); ever bearing, which produces a few littler harvests for every season; and day impartial, which persistently sets modest quantities of strawberries all through the season.

  Strawberry plants like to spread by means of sprinters. In any case, for the best natural product creation, limit the sprinters to only a couple of plants and prune the rest. Additionally, squeeze off the blooms in a plant's first season to keep it from fruiting. This will permit it to put its vitality toward building up a sound root framework, which will altogether expand its yield the following season. At last, hope to replace or revive your strawberry plant every 5 years.

- **Raspberry and blackberry.** Raspberries and blackberries have consistently been the patio's top choices. In any case, some seasoned assortments can be unruly plants, spreading broadly and being canvassed in thistles that made harvesting a rather difficult task. In addition, planting a blend of them right on time, mid-season, and late-season assortments will increase your harvest for quite a long time.

The plants do require yearly pruning to keep them profitable, yet it is a fast activity. The objective of pruning is to thin the plants enough that light and air can arrive at all parts. This advantages in development and assists with forestalling different diseases.

- **Green grapes.** In spite of the fact that grapevines are not hard to develop, you will confront solid rivalry at various times from winged animals and different creatures. In addition, grapes need some kind of trellis or backing to develop. There is additionally a lot of proposals on the most proficient method to prune them. However, numerous individuals develop them effectively with a loose drew closer to pruning.

Check with your nearby gardening nursery or office to find out about the best grape assortments for your territory. Furthermore, make an effort to note whether an assortment is best for eating or winemaking. Most grape assortments need a bright area with rich soil that has great seepage and air dissemination to forestall morbidity.

- **Red cherries.** Cherries are one of the least demanding organic products to develop and think about. They require

95

negligible to no pruning and are once in a while tormented by bugs or illnesses. Sweet fruits need 2 trees for cross-fertilization except if you plant a tree with 2 distinct assortments united on it. Besides, you can pull off only one tree when you are developing these fruits.

Prune your cherry plant in the winter while it is as yet lethargic, and prepare it in the late winter. Additionally, these trees aren't very welcoming to the dry season. So, guarantee that they get watering or precipitation at any rate week by week or more during the blistering climate.

- **Melons**. If by any chance you aren't prepared for the effort of planting a tree or a bush, you can, in any case, develop heavenly melons in your nursery or in compartments. Melons need a great deal of sun and warmth.

They additionally require sufficient space, as they develop on vines that can undoubtedly arrive at 20 feet or more. It is conceivable to develop melons on a trellis, yet you should pick an assortment with little natural products. Huge melons, for example, watermelon, can turn out to be heavy to such an extent that they will drop off from the plants.

Plant your melons after the risk of snow has gone for the season. Water it consistently as they develop and get built up. At that point, when the natural products begin to show up, you can ease off watering them.

Growing Flowers in Raised Bed Garden

Planting in raised beds is essentially a hybrid method for cultivating your plants. It is half compartment planting and half raised bed cultivating. Customary raised beds come up short on a base and are genuinely huge in size, while compartments have a base to contain the soil and are far smaller than a raised bed. In case you're searching for a more straightforward method to cultivate, raised bed planting may simply be your new closest companion. With this procedure, you can gather tons of foods grown from the ground, armloads of roses, and unlimited bundles of herbs with negligible exertion.

If you have generally longed for having a stunning blooming garden, right now is an ideal opportunity to get it going. Beginning a flower garden is both amusing and fulfilling. Follow the rules for novices mentioned next, and your garden will look extraordinary.

Some bloom seeds, for example, sunflowers, can be planted easily when the ground defrosts (it is better to have a look at the packet of the seed for further instructions). Many gardeners, as a rule, start a couple of sorts of blossoms indoors as a good head start. When growing, keep in mind to effectively hold the stemmed marvels ahead of schedule as could reasonably be expected with the goal that blossoms don't tumble in a solid breeze or from the heaviness of their sprouts.

Following are the rules that need to be followed while raising flowers in a raised bed:

- The initial phase in making the ideal blossom garden is to acquaint yourself with the zone in which you need to grow the flowers. Be straightforward with light, dampness conditions, and the size of the location.

- A significant hint to guarantee an effective bloom garden is to have a dirt test done for your soil and utilize the outcome to revise your soil before growing your flowers.

- To ensure your recently planted nursery will endure the seasons, you should know your region's normal last and first snow dates. Beginning your seeds around 1 ½ month before the normal last snowing date will give your plants a kick-off. The flowers will bloom quicker and have very low weed growth.

- Take time at assembling various shapes and check whether they sparkle off one another. A few mixes will be energetic and dynamic, and others may conflict. Planting comparative blossom shapes together can be very helpful.

- Plants you choose ought to have a long season, and not look messy in the wake of blooming and thrive in the provided nursery's conditions. For a progressively beneficial bloom garden, it is recommended to empower longer stems as this will lessen weeds and enhance the number of blossoms.

- In the event that you need your blossoms to overflow in a characteristic manner, yet don't need them close enough for the trimmer's cutting edges, introduce square shapes of flagstone around the beds. Additionally, keep ways between blossom beds wide enough, so blossoms won't be stomped all over when strolling through the nursery.

- Increase pruning work and planting bushes at the focal point of your blossom beds to give all-year structure and tallness.

Advantages of Growing Flowers in a Raised Bed

Flower gardens are being enjoyed by the world since it has numerous advantages. Additionally, having lovely shading, blossoms are likewise efficient and cost-effective. Indeed, blossom plants are loved and appreciated by people belonging to all age groups. Here is a fair portion of advantages we can acquire by planting blossoms:

- The nearness of plants pulls in fascination since it looks delightful. Blossoms can be a fancy medium both in and out of the room or the house. Different shades of blooming plants can enhance the beauty of the room, the roads, and also nature. Assorted flower plants together can make the garden a lot more fascinating, increasingly noticeable, and develop a feeling of pride.

- Flower plants can develop a positive air with the goal that people will feel more joyful, prosperous, and have some mental peace when watching these blooming plants. An individual can transform into a more calm and cheerful person when being around these blossoms. The presence of these plants can change an individual's feelings. Consequently, if you are feeling occupied, tired with regular issues, going to the nursery or gardens full of flowers in a recreation center may prove to be the correct bidder to fix your state of mind.

- Growing blossoms is very advantageous to the earth. Flowering plants can likewise decrease air contamination in the earth. At the point when the flower plants experience the procedure of photosynthesis, the leaves ingest carbon dioxide and discharge oxygen. Oxygen is required by every single living thing to live and relax. In fact, blooming plants can decrease the event of soil disintegration in light of the fact that the flowering plants can hold the soil pretty well.

There is a large number of advantages that flowers have for you and the earth around your home. You may think of adding this increasingly wonderful and loveable addition to your home.

Best Flowers to Be Grown in a Raised Bed Garden

Having flowers in the vegetable nursery can diminish pest issues and improve biodiversity. Here are some exceptionally well-grown flowers to develop for sound nursery crops. Many specialists urge gardeners to plant an outskirt of blossoms around the border of the nursery.

Likewise, the specialists urge to plant the accompanying blossoms among the harvests. This can pull in helpful creepy pets legitimately to where they're needed. That's on the grounds that in a permaculture garden, this training incorporates various parts of the nursery to make the general biological system more diverse, productive, and less needy of support.

Further, it's not just over-the-ground bugs that beautiful flowers can help with. Blossoms additionally help to keep up a solid nursery environment by holding the soil set up and by taking care of the valuable soil creatures.

Following is the rundown of some beautiful as well as useful flowers to be grown:

- **Calendula**: It may very well be a preferred yearly flower to develop in the vegetable nursery. These flowers can be grown annually with a sprightly, yellow, daisy-like bloom to about 18–24-inch tall. It oozes a clingy sap that traps bugs like aphids and whiteflies and keeps them off of close-by crops.

  It pulls in numerous kinds of pollinators and advantageous bugs like ladybugs and green lacewings which appreciate the bloom nectar, yet additionally, attract their most loved pests. Calendula can even be developed like a spread yield over the winter to hold up the soil.

- **California poppy**: These flowers tend to grow a lot quicker than all flowers, you plant it one day and you will observe growth in a few days. It is captivated by the deep roots of this plant which mines the earth's soil and mellows it, just as the brilliant yellow blossoms that reveal to you when it will rain for the day. The fancy foliage of the flowers is mostly loved by useful insects. For these reasons, you can begin planting it in your vegetable nursery and be delighted in the excellence and sound vegetable harvests. These flowers will develop to around 12-inch.

- **German chamomile:** These are charming and humble flowers with their elegant foliage that pulls in pollinators and helpful insects. Growing to around 12-inch, chamomile is a grassland plant that has roots so deep which digs up supplements.

- **Nasturtium**: This is a yearly flower that has peppery leaves and blossoms. Emitting a solid aroma, it repulses creepy pests. Its thick, low-developing propensity (12–18-inch) makes it a fantastic living mulch as it covers the soil underneath taller harvests, and feeds the soil as it bites the dust back. The flashy blossoms and foliage are most loved in the consumable scene.

- **Sweet Alyssum**: It is a low-developing plant that is prevalently developed in scene outskirts. It has a lovely aroma. In spite of the fact that there are numerous hues to browse, the white blossoms draw in the most valuable creepy pests. Significant numbers of hoverflies are observed when you plant sweet alyssum flowers in the nursery.

7. Tried and Tested Recipes: From Your Garden to Your Table the Gardening

There's no better feeling than using home-grown ingredients in your cooking—that feeling of satisfaction of knowing that you successfully planted and harvested your own crops and now you get to cook with them is second to none. This chapter will provide you with recipes. These recipes will include ones for preservation such as pickling and canning recipes along with recipes for everyday meals that you can make with the fresh produce from your garden.

Grilled Garden Vegetables

Ingredients

- 8 small carrots with 1-inch greens intact, peeled

- 6 green onions, cut into 3-inch pieces

- 2 medium red and/or yellow bell peppers, cut into 8 wedges

- 2 medium zucchini and/or yellow squash, cut diagonally into 1-inch pieces

- 2 tbsps. butter, melted

- 1 tsp. finely chopped fresh garlic

- ½ tsp. coarse ground pepper

- ¼ tsp. salt

Directions

1. Heat your grill to medium or prepare your charcoal grill—your charcoal grill will be ready when the coals are ash white.

2. Create a bowl out of aluminum foil and put the carrots, onions, bell peppers, and squash into it.

3. Drizzle melted butter onto your vegetables and sprinkle them with garlic, ground pepper, and salt.

4. Put the aluminum bowl onto the grill and cover it. Allow your vegetables to grill for about 8–12 minutes (or until vegetables are cooked).

Notes: Serve with lightly spiced rice and grilled or roasted chicken.

Basil Pesto

Ingredients

- ½ clove garlic

- 1 big bunch of fresh basil

- 1 handful of pine nuts, lightly toasted

- 1 handful of freshly grated Parmesan cheese

- Extra-virgin olive oil as needed

- 1 lemon (optional)

- Sea salt and black pepper to taste

Directions

1. Peel the garlic and grind with a pestle and mortar with a pinch of sea salt. Alternatively, put the garlic and sea salt into a food processor and pulse.

2. Pick fresh basil leaves from your garden and roughly chop them. Add the basil leaves to the garlic mix in your processor or pestle and mortar and either process or mash the mixture until it forms a paste.

3. Once you have your garlic and basil paste, you can add the pine nuts. For a deeper taste, lightly toast your pine nuts first. Once you have added the pine nuts, process or mash the mixture again. Stir in half of the required parmesan cheese.

4. Pour some oil into the mixture – you do not need a lot of oil, just enough to bind the ingredients and form a slightly runny paste consistency.

5. You now have delicious basil pesto! You can add the remaining cheese and season with salt and black pepper to your taste. If the consistency becomes too pasty then you can add some more oil.

Notes: Serve on toasted bread, use on pizzas, or mix into salad dressing. Add a dash of lemon to the mix if you'd like a slightly tangy pesto.

Marinara Sauce

Ingredients

- 3 tbsps. olive oil

- 1 cup onion, finely diced

- ⅓ cup carrot, shredded

- 3 garlic cloves, minced

- ¼ cup fresh basil, chopped

- ½ tsp. dried oregano

- Salt and pepper to taste

- 28 oz. whole tomatoes, canned

- 28 oz. crushed tomatoes, canned

- 2 tbsps. tomato paste

- 1–2 tsps. sugar (optional)

- ½ cup water

Directions

1. Turn your stove to medium and place olive oil into a large pot. Put the large pot onto the stove and add onions, carrots, and garlic. Cook the vegetables for 5 minutes or until the vegetables no longer have a fresh crunch.

2. As soon as your vegetables are cooked, add in whole tomatoes (with juice) and gently break the tomatoes apart with a wooden spoon. Allow this mixture to cook for a few minutes before you stir in the rest of the ingredients.

3. Bring the sauce to a gentle boil then lower the heat and simmer with no lid for approximately 20 minutes. If you like thicker marinara sauce, cook for longer.

4. Allow the marinara sauce to cool slightly before packing into a container to either freeze or keep in the fridge for the week.

Notes: You can serve this marinara sauce over spaghetti or use it as a sauce for your pizzas.

Mint Tea

Ingredients

- Boiling water

- Honey

- Fresh mint leaves

Directions

1. Boil the kettle and then pour the water into a cup or mug of your choice.

2. Break a few mint leaves and add to the hot water. Throw some whole fresh mint leaves and honey into your cup.

3. Mix with a spoon until the honey dissolves and then let the mint leaves steep for 3–5 minutes. You can strain the tea and drink it or simply drink it with the leaves.

Lemongrass Lemon Bars With Coconut Shortbread Crust

Ingredients

- 1 ¾ cups all-purpose flour

- 1 cup sweetened shredded coconut

- ½ cup powdered sugar

- ½ cup butter, room temperature + 3 tbsps.

- 1 ¼ cups sugar

- 2 lemongrass stalks, bottom 4-inch roughly chopped with the tough outer layer removed

- 5 tbsps. lemon juice, fresh

- 3 eggs, large

- 1 tsp. vanilla extract

- Powdered sugar to sprinkle on top

- Salt to taste

Directions

1. Preheat the oven to 350°F.

2. Butter or use nonstick spray on a 13-by-9-inch metal baking pan. Set aside while you prepare the crust.

3. Beat 1 ½ cups of flour, coconut, powdered sugar, and ½ tsp. salt in a large bowl until well blended. You can do this by hand or with an electric mixer.

4. Put the butter and vanilla into the bowl once the dry ingredients above have been mixed and then beat (on low speed if using an electric mixer) until little moist clusters begin to form.

5. Once the clusters begin to form, tip the contents of the bowl into the baking pan. Press the dough until smooth and even in the pan.

6. Bake the crust until it looks golden brown. This should take approximately 25 minutes, however, start checking from the 20-minute mark so you do not burn your crust. Take your crust out if your filling is not done when the crust is.

7. While your crust is baking, mix the sugar and lemongrass together. You will need a food processor for this step. Pulse the lemongrass and sugar until the lemongrass is ground finely.

8. Once the lemongrass is ground finely and incorporated well with the sugar, add in lemon juice and process until thoroughly mixed.

9. Crack your eggs and add them to the food processor. Blend for 10–15 seconds so the egg can be incorporated.

10. Add ¼ cup of flour and salt and process until the mixture is smooth.

11. Once your crust is done and your filling is done—take the crust out of the oven and place it on the counter to cool ever so slightly.

12. Decrease the oven's temperature to 320°F.

13. Pour the filling over the hot crust and then pop it back into the oven. Bake until the filling is firm—this can take anywhere from 20–25 minutes. Once cooked, remove the pan from the oven and allow the bars to cool in the pan.

14. Cut into pieces and serve with a dusting of powdered sugar.

Notes: This serves 8–10 people. Baking times may vary depending on your oven.

Mexican Bean Stew

Ingredients

- Low-calorie cooking spray

- 1 onion, thinly sliced

- 2 garlic cloves, crushed

- 1 yellow pepper, deseeded and cut into 1-inch chunks

- ½ tsp. hot chili powder

- 1 tsp. ground cumin

- 1 tsp. ground coriander

- 14 oz. can chopped tomatoes

- 2 tbsp. tomato purée

- 14 oz. can of mixed beans, drained and rinsed

- 10 oz. water, cold

- 4 ½ oz. whole-grain long-grain rice, to serve

- 3 ½ oz. fat-free Greek yogurt, to serve

- 1 lime, cut into wedges, to serve

- Salt and freshly ground black pepper

For the salsa:

- 1 tomato, roughly chopped

- 4 tbsp. roughly chopped fresh coriander

- 2 spring onions, thinly sliced

Directions

1. Turn the stove to medium heat and place a large thick-based frying pan on the heat. Add oil and once heated, add the onion and garlic. Cook for about 3 minutes, then add pepper and continue cooking for 2 minutes.

2. Toss in the spices and braise for a few seconds. Add the tomatoes, tomato purée, and mixed beans into the pot and then add over 10 oz. cold water and bring to a gentle boil. Once boiling, add salt and ground pepper.

3. Lower the heat and allow to simmer for 30 minutes, stirring occasionally until the stew has thickened.

4. While your stew is cooking, make your rice. Boil water in your kettle then transfer to the pot or bring the water to a boil in a medium-sized pot. Add rice and let boil for 25 minutes. Keep an eye on the water levels and top up with

hot water if your water runs low. Once the rice is tender, turn the stove off and strain the rice. Stir occasionally to prevent the rice from sticking to the bottom of the pot.

5. Once your stew and rice are finished, make your salsa. To make the salsa, mix the tomato, coriander, and spring onions together in a bowl.

6. Dish rice and then ladle the beans on top. Dish salsa on the side or on top of your rice and beans. Serve with plain yogurt and lime wedges.

Vinegar Carrots

Ingredients

- 2 carrots, julienned

- Vinegar to cover the carrots

- Green chilies, sliced in half

Directions

1. Put the carrots and chilies into a jar and then top with vinegar.

2. Allow this mixture to sit for at least 2 days before eating it.

Grilled Corn

Ingredients

- 4 ears of sweetcorn, cleaned

- Butter, for serving

- Kosher salt

- Any other seasonings of your choice

Directions

There are many ways to cook corn! You can grill it on your barbecue stand, use your oven grill, or use a grill pan. Follow these simple instructions to get the tastiest grilled corn you can imagine.

Barbecue stand:

1. If you are having a barbecue, you can grill corn in 2 ways—you can either steam the corn and then place the corn on high heat for a few minutes to singe it or you can put the uncooked corn on the barbecue when the flame is of medium heat and let it cook for approximately 10–15 minutes or until it is grilled to your taste.

2. Smear the corn with butter and top with salt and your choice of spice. Devour with gusto!

Oven grilled:

1. Preheat your oven to 425°F.

2. Make little boats with aluminum foil and tuck your corn cobs into the little boats.

3. Mix 4 dollops of butter with salt and spice (if you are using any) and then place a dollop of spiced or salted butter into each boat.

4. Close the "boats" and put the corn into the oven.

5. Cook for 20–25 minutes or until soft. Cooking times will vary depending on the size of your corn and the power of your oven.

6. Once the corn is cooked soft, you can char the corn by opening up the little boats and placing the bare corn on the grill until it is browned or blackened.

7. Break into smaller pieces and enjoy with roasted chicken or simply eat as it.

Stovetop:

1. Turn the stove to medium-high.

2. Place a thick base or griller pan on the stove to heat while you mix butter and salt or spice and then smear onto corn.

3. Place the corn into the pan and cook for 15–20 minutes. Turn the corn frequently to ensure even cooking.

4. Once the corn has been cooked, turn the stove to high and char according to your preference. Personally, I prefer mine nicely browned. I then add another dollop of spicy butter.

Notes: Spices that you can use for your grilled corn include pepper, chives, parsley, garlic flakes, or thyme.

Canned Berries

This recipe can work with blackberries, blueberries, currants, dewberries, gooseberries, huckleberries, loganberries, mulberries, raspberries.

Ingredients

For the blackberry juice:

- 2 cups blackberries, divided

- ¼ cup water

For the canned blackberries:

- 2 cups water

- 2 cups sugar

- 1 cinnamon stick

- ½ tsp. nutmeg, preferably freshly grated

- 4 cups berries

- ½ cup brandy (optional, substitute with an equal amount of juice)

- Blackberry juice prepared above

- 2 (1 pint) jars or 4 (½ pint) jars

Directions

1. Prepare your canning jars by ensuring that they are washed clean and dried completely. Once prepared, keep your jars within easy reach and begin preparing a water bath for canning.

2. To prepare your water bath, you need to have a tall pot and a rack that will fit inside of the pot. Place the rack inside the pot. The rack will aid in providing even heat distribution and will prevent your jars from knocking against each other and cracking. Fill the pot with enough water to cover the jars you are using. Turn the stove on and heat the water until it is 180°F. Use a thermometer to test the temperature. If you heat the water too much, you may cause your jars to crack.

3. To begin preparing your canned berries, chuck the berries into a small pot or saucepan. Stamp the berries down with a potato masher—you do not want a puree, you just want to fragment the berries. Pour ¼ cup of water into the pot with the berries and allow to simmer gently for about 2 minutes. The berries will release their juices. Turn off the heat and strain the mixture. Keep the juice and the berries separately. We are going to use the berry juice for the

canning. You can use the mashed berries for baking or cooking.

4. In another saucepan or pot, add 2 cups of water, sugar, and spices. Bring this mixture to a boil. Once the mixture begins to boil, lower the heat and allow to simmer for 3–5 minutes. Add in the rest of the berries, the brandy, and the berry juice.

5. Bring the berry, spice, and brandy mixture to boil. Stir constantly to prevent scorching and to distribute the heat evenly. Use a wooden spoon and stir gently to prevent breaking your berries too much. Allow this mixture to boil for 1–2 minutes.

6. Once your berry, spice, and brandy mixture has boiled, turn off the heat and use a slotted spoon to fill your canning jars with blackberries. Leave a generous space of about ½-inch empty.

7. You can either pour or dish the berry syrup over the fruits. Make sure you cover the fruits. You still need to ensure that you keep some space empty when filling the jar with the juices.

8. Wipe the jars' rims clean and then close them.

9. Place the jars into the water bath for 10 minutes. Once 10 minutes is up, turn off the heat and wait for 5 minutes before taking the jars out of the pot. Place the jars onto a cloth on the counter. Using a cloth will prevent your jars from cracking if your countertops are very cold. Leave the jars to cool down.

10. After a day or so, check the seals by tapping on each jar's lid—the lids should not move up and down when pressed, they should feel firm and concave. If some of your jars don't seal, put them into the fridge and use them within 3 days.

Notes: Most berries can be used by following this process—you can adjust the spices depending on what flavor profile you are looking for. The berries used for juice can be reused for any purpose such as baking berry muffins.

Garden Soup

Ingredients

- 4 tbsps. olive oil

- 2 tbsps. garlic, finely minced

- 2 cups chopped leeks, white part only, requires around 3 leeks

- Kosher salt

- 2 cups fresh green beans, cut into ¾-inch pieces

- 2 cups carrots, peeled and chopped into rounds

- 2 cups peeled and diced potatoes

- 2 quarts chicken or vegetable broth

- 4 cups peeled, seeded, and chopped tomatoes

- Kernels from 2 ears of corn

- ½ tsp. black pepper, freshly ground

- ¼ cup packed, chopped fresh parsley leaves

- 1–2 tsps. lemon juice, freshly squeezed

Directions

1. Turn your stove to medium or low. Place a thick-based pot on the stove with some olive oil. You are going to make soup in this pot so make sure the pot is big enough. Once your olive oil is hot, add the leeks, garlic, and a touch of salt. Cook for 7–8 minutes or until the leeks and garlic begin to soften. You will know that they are softening when they look limp. If you want, you can taste it—there should be no crunch when you chew.

2. Once your leeks and garlic are softened, add in the carrots, potatoes, and green beans. Stir frequently to keep your vegetables from sticking or burning. Cook for 4–5 minutes.

3. If you are using stock cakes (powdered stock), mix the stock with water and then pour it into the pot. If you are using liquid stock, just pour it into the pot. Bring to a gentle boil. Stir to keep the vegetables from sticking and burning. Simmer for about 3–5 minutes. Then throw in your tomatoes, corn kernels, and pepper. Stir to incorporate well.

4. Reduce the heat to low. Cover the pot and cook until all the vegetables are soft. This should take between 25–30 minutes. You can test the vegetables by tasting them after

25 minutes. If the vegetables still have a crunch to them, then the soup needs to cook more.

5. Once your vegetables are soft, take the pot off of the heat. Sprinkle parsley and drizzle lemon juice into the soup. Shake some salt onto the soup and serve immediately. Bon appetit!

Greek Salad

Ingredients

For the dressing:

- ¼ cup extra-virgin olive oil

- 3 tbsps. red wine vinegar

- 1 garlic clove, minced

- ½ tsp. dried oregano, more for sprinkling

- ¼ tsp. Dijon mustard

- ¼ tsp. sea salt

- Freshly ground black pepper

For the salad:

- 1 English cucumber, cut lengthwise, seeded, and sliced ¼-inch thick

- 1 green bell pepper, chopped into 1-inch pieces

- 2 cups halved cherry tomatoes

- 5 oz. feta cheese, cut into ½-inch cubes

- ⅓ cup thinly sliced red onion

- ⅓ cup pitted Kalamata olives

- ⅓ cup fresh mint leaves

Directions

1. To make the dressing: Mix together all the ingredients for the salad dressing until well incorporated.

2. To make the salad: Put all salad ingredients into a serving bowl. Toss to get all your veggies mixed. When you dish the salad, you'll want to get a little bit of everything, not just the cucumbers or peppers so make sure you toss well!

3. Drizzle salad dressing onto the salad. Toss again but gently this time so that you don't get the dressing all over the floor! Top with some oregano and mint leaves.

Notes: This salad can be eaten on its own or served as an accompaniment to barbecued food. You can also add some chicken or grilled fish to this salad to make it a meal on its own.

Onion Soup

Ingredients

- ½ cup butter, unsalted

- 2 tbsps. olive oil

- 4 cups onions, sliced

- 4 (10 ½ oz.) cans of beef broth

- 2 tbsps. dry sherry, optional

- 1 tsp. dried thyme

- Salt and pepper as desired

- 4 slices bread, toasted

- 4 slices Provolone cheese, sliced

- 2 slices Swiss cheese, sliced

- ¼ cup Parmesan cheese, grated

Directions

1. Turn the stove to medium and melt the butter with olive oil in a thick-based pot that can hold about 8 quarts of liquid.

2. Once the butter is melted, put your onions into the pot and stir continuously until the onions are caramelized. You will know that the onions are caramelized when they turn a deep golden brown. This process takes time so do not try and rush it or you will risk burning the onions. The key to great-tasting caramelized onions is to slow cook them.

3. As soon as the onions are caramelized, add beef broth, sherry (if using), and thyme. Season with salt and pepper. Bring the mixture to boil by raising the heat, and then lower the heat once the mixture has boiled so that it can simmer for about 30 minutes.

4. Heat the oven broiler.

5. Pour or dish the soup into oven-safe serving bowls or an oven-safe casserole dish.

6. Layer whole or broken toast on top of the soup and top with cheeses. You should place 1 slice of Provolone, ½ slice of Swiss cheese, and 1 tbsp. Parmesan cheese if you are using individual bowls. If using a big casserole dish, simply place the cheese on top in a ratio of 1-½-1.

7. Take your bowl and put it onto an oven tray—broil until the cheeses bubble and brown. Brown to your desire. I

personally prefer lightly browned cheese while my partner likes it slightly more browned.

Herb Omelette

Ingredients

- 4 eggs

- 1 tbsp. chopped chives

- 1 tbsp. chopped dill

- 2 tbsps. mascarpone cheese

- 3 tbsps. butter

- Salt to taste

Directions

1. Put the stove on low and start preheating a saucepan. Put the butter into the saucepan. While waiting for the butter to melt, begin step 2.

2. Blend together all of the ingredients, except the butter. Beat the mixture until it is homogenized.

3. As soon as the butter is melted, you can tip the omelet mix into the frying pan. Cook over low heat. Once the eggs begin to set—this is when the egg starts solidifying—then you can slide the spatula under the egg so you can loosen the edges.

4. Angle the pan so that any raw egg can run to the side. Another way to cook your eggs is to poke holes in your omelet and close the pan so that the steam can cook your eggs.

5. If you want to add filling to your omelet, you can do so once your omelet is 90% cooked. Place the filling in the middle of the omelet.

6. Once your omelet is completely cooked, slide the spatula underneath the omelet carefully so that you can tip the edges onto the center to fold from opposite ends of your omelet.

7. Dish the omelet onto a plate and serve with toast and grilled cherry tomatoes.

Notes: Fillings for your omelet can include cheese, bacon, mushrooms, artichokes, and aubergines, or any combination thereof. Alternatively, you can add any filling you desire.

Dried Fruit Pickle

Ingredients

- 4.4 oz. apricot

- 4.4 oz. dried figs

- 3 cups vinegar

- 3 tsp. chili powder

- 2 tsp. salt

- 4.4 oz. dates—can substitute with peach or prune

- 4.4 oz. seedless raisins

- 12.4 oz. Jaggery

Directions

1. Put the apricots and dates into half a cup of vinegar and soak overnight. In the morning, drain the vinegar and remove the seeds. Chop the fruits in halves or quarters. If you are using prunes, do not soak them in vinegar.

2. Grate the jaggery.

3. Tip the jaggery, remaining vinegar, salt, and chili powder into a large enamel pot and bring the mixture to a boil. This

can take anywhere from 5–15 minutes depending on the power of your stove. Once the mixture has reached boiling point, allow it to boil for 5 minutes. Gently throw the fruit into the pot and let boil for another 5 minutes.

4. After boiling the fruit for 5 minutes, decrease the heat, and keep the mixture on heat until the mixture thickens. Stir frequently to prevent scorching.

5. Once the mixture has thickened, remove the pot from heat and allow it to cool before bottling.

Notes: This can be eaten on its own or served as a side with food.

Garlic in Oil

Ingredients

- 3–5 heads of garlic

- Enough olive oil to cover the garlic (you can substitute with sunflower oil)

Directions

1. Separate heads into individual cloves of garlic.

2. Peel the garlic cloves. You can leave the cloves whole, chop, or mince them.

3. Place garlic cloves in a small jar that has a tight-fitting lid and cover with oil.

4. The garlic cloves should be completely covered.

5. Store in the refrigerator for up to 3 months.

6. Replenish oil as needed to keep the garlic covered.

Notes: You can add whole, minced, or chopped chilies to your garlic to make chili garlic. The longer garlic stays in the oil, the stronger it will taste. You can use the oil from the garlic to give dishes a light garlic flavor.

Beef Stew

Ingredients

- 3 lbs. boneless beef chuck, chopped into ½–1-inch pieces

- 2 tsps. salt

- 1 tsp. black pepper, freshly ground

- 3 tbsps. olive oil

- 2 medium yellow onions, sliced into 1-inch chunks

- 7 cloves garlic, peeled and smashed

- 2 tbsps. balsamic vinegar

- 1 ½ tbsps. tomato paste

- ¼ cup all-purpose flour

- 2 cups dry red wine

- 2 cups water

- 2 cups beef broth

- ½ tsp. dried thyme

- 1 bay leaf

- 1 ½ tsps. sugar

- 4 large carrots, peeled and cut diagonally into 1-inch pieces

- 1 lb. small white potatoes, cut in half

- Fresh chopped parsley, for serving, optional

Directions

1. Preheat the oven to 325°F and place the rack in the lower-middle position.

2. Dry your beef by patting it with a serviette or cloth. Add salt and pepper according to your preference.

3. In a large Dutch oven or a thick-based soup pot, heat 1 tbsp. olive oil on medium-high heat. After the olive oil starts to shimmer and shine, toss the meat into the pot and fry until the meat is nicely browned. You will need to fry the meat in at least 3 batches so that it can fry properly.

4. Use tongs to turn the meat chunks and allow each batch of meat to fry for about 5 minutes. Add more olive oil as necessary. In order for the meat to brown properly, you should not overcrowd the pan.

5. Once browned, transfer the meat to a large plate, cover it with a net, and leave it on the counter.

6. Into the same pot that you used to brown the meat, add the onions, garlic, and balsamic vinegar. Using the same pot will keep all of the flavors and give them a chance to amalgamate. Cook the onions and garlic for about 5 minutes. Then squeeze the tomato paste into the pan and cook for another minute.

7. By the time your onion, garlic, and tomato mix is done, the beef that has been resting will have released some juices onto the plate. Reserve some beef juices for step 8. Throw the beef and most of its juices into the pot.

8. Mix some of the beef juices with the flour to form a paste. Mix with a whisk or fork until the flour paste is thoroughly mixed with no lumps. Then pour the paste into the beef mixture and stir with a wooden spoon until the paste is dissolved and incorporated. Allow it to cook for a few minutes before adding the wine, water, beef broth, thyme, bay leaf, and sugar.

9. Stir well and then bring the pot to a boil. Once the pot has boiled, cover the pot with a lid and then transfer the pot to the oven and allow it to cook for 2 hours.

10. After 2 hours in the oven, take the pot out and add the carrots and potatoes. Re-cover and put the pot back into the oven for another hour.

11. Once 1 hour has passed, check to see whether the stew is ready. You will know it is done when the vegetables are soft, the broth has thickened, and the meat is nicely tender.

12. Find the bay leaf, take it out of your stew, and then season to taste with salt and pepper.

13. Serve immediately or let it come to room temperature and then store in the refrigerator overnight or until ready to serve. The taste of this stew improves the longer it is left to soak in the flavors. The best time to serve this stew would be the next day. Reheat the stew in a covered pot on your stove over medium heat or at 350°F in the oven.

Notes: This stew can be made freezer-friendly with a few adjustments and can be frozen for up to 3 months. Omit the potatoes as they don't freeze well. If you'd like, you can boil some potatoes separately and add them the day you defrost the stew or you can serve them on the side. To defrost the stew, you can leave it in the fridge for 1 day and then reheat on the stove over medium-low heat until hot or leave it on the counter to defrost.

Cherry Pie

Ingredients

- 2 pie crusts (1 for bottom and 1 for top)

- 4 ½ cups halved pitted fresh cherries

- ⅔ cup granulated sugar

- ¼ cup cornstarch

- 1 tbsp. lemon juice

- 1 tsp. pure vanilla extract

- ¼ tsp. almond extract

- 1 tbsp. unsalted butter, cold and cut into small cubes

- Egg wash: 1 large egg beaten with 1 tbsp. milk

- Coarse sugar to sprinkle on crust, optional

Directions

1. To make the filling, mix the cherries, sugar, cornstarch, lemon juice, vanilla, and almond extract in a large bowl until they are thoroughly combined. Leave the filling in the refrigerator while you preheat the oven. This gives the filling a chance to rest.

2. Preheat the oven to 400°F.

3. If you are using homemade pastry, chill the dough and roll it out on top of a floured surface. Spin the dough around frequently using the tips of your fingers to help it spread out. If your dough does not move easily, do not force the 'spin,' instead, lift the dough up and flour the surface well before resuming your rolling. Once you have a circle that is about 12-inch in diameter you can carefully lift the dough and place it into a 9-by-2-inch pie dish. Tuck the pastry into the tin by pressing it against the insides with your fingers. Make sure that it is smooth—If using ready rolled, place 1 pastry into your baking tin.

4. Use a slotted spoon to dish the filling into the crust. Do not put a lot of juice into the pie as it will make the pie soggy. Throw any leftover juices away.

5. Place chunks of butter on top of the filling.

6. Take the other piece of dough from the fridge to make the top. If using homemade dough, roll the dough into a circle that is about 12-inch in diameter. Using a pastry wheel, pizza cutter, or sharp knife, cut the dough into strips. Carefully thread the strips over and under one another to weave the covering of your pie. Once completed, press the edges of the strips and the bottom pie crust together to

form a seal. Trim off any excess dough from your pie. Use the excess dough for small jam tarts.

7. Once your pie is constructed, it is ready for baking. Crack an egg and whisk it for a minute. Take a pastry brush and brush the top of the pie crust with the egg. Sprinkle the top with coarse sugar, if desired.

8. Place the pie onto a large baking sheet and bake for 20 minutes. The baking tray underneath your pie will keep spills in your oven to a minimum if your pie bubbles. After 20 minutes, simply turn the heat down to 375°F and bake for an additional 30–35 minutes.

9. Before serving, allow the pie to cool for 3 hours at room temperature to allow the filling to thicken.

10. Cover any leftovers tightly with cling wrap and store in the refrigerator for up to 5 days.

Notes: Keep everything as cold as possible to maintain a nice fresh taste. Also, don't rush the cooling process at the end as otherwise, you will end up with a runny, unsatisfying pie.

Stuffed Bell Peppers

Ingredients

- 6 bell peppers, any color

- 4 tbsps. olive oil, plus more for drizzling

- 8 oz. lean ground beef

- Kosher salt

- Black pepper, freshly ground

- 1 onion, finely diced

- 2 cloves garlic, chopped

- 1 medium zucchini, finely diced

- 4 Roma tomatoes, seeded and finely diced

- Red pepper flakes, as desired

- 1 cup cooked long-grain and wild rice

- 1 ½ cups grated pepper Jack cheese

Directions

1. Start by turning your oven to 350°F and your stovetop to medium-high.

2. Wash your peppers and then cut off the tops. Take out the stems and seeds. Discard those.

3. Chop the tops finely and set them aside—these will go into your mix in step 8.

4. Place the peppers cut-side up in a baking dish that is just the right size to hold them upright—do not use a dish that is too big or your peppers may fall over.

5. Place a large skillet onto the hot stove and heat 2 tbsps. olive oil.

6. Once the olive oil is heated, add the beef and seasoning. Break up the lumps by separating the meat with a wooden spoon and keep the meat on the heat until it is cooked through and browning. This should take about 10 minutes.

7. Dish the beef into a bowl that is lined with a paper towel.

8. Add another 2 tbsps. olive oil into your skillet and then add the onions and chopped pepper tops. Cook until they soften, this can take between 3–4 minutes.

9. Throw the garlic and zucchini into the skillet and cook for another minute.

10. Next, throw in the tomatoes and flavor with salt and red pepper flakes to taste.

11. Keep the skillet on the heat until everything is warmed, then mix in the beef and the rice. Taste and season as needed. Add 1 cup of cheese to the rice and beef mixture.

12. Now for the fun part! Start filling the peppers with the rice mixture and then top with a generous amount of cheese.

13. Put some water into the bottom of the baking dish to allow the outsides of your peppers to steam and prevent them from drying out.

14. Drizzle the peppers with olive oil and then cover your peppers with foil. Bake for 30 minutes.

15. After 30 minutes, take the foil off of the peppers and then bake the peppers for another 15–20 minutes. You will know that the peppers are ready when the cheese has melted and the peppers are soft.

Bacon Macaroni Salad

Ingredients

- 2 cups elbow macaroni, uncooked

- 1 tomato, large and finely chopped

- 5 green onions, finely chopped

- 2 celery ribs, finely chopped

- 1 ¼ cups mayonnaise

- 5 tsps. white vinegar

- ⅛–¼ tsp. pepper

- ¼ tsp. salt

- 1 lb. bacon strips, cooked and crumbled

Directions

1. Bring water to boil and cook the macaroni (or any other pasta if you'd like) according to the manufacturer's instructions.

2. Once the pasta is cooked al dente, strain and rinse with cold water.

3. Tip the pasta into a large bowl and add the tomato, green onions, and celery. Mix well so that the ingredients are evenly distributed.

4. In a small bowl, whisk mayonnaise, vinegar, salt, and pepper until combined thoroughly.

5. Pour this mixture over the macaroni mixture and toss it like a salad to coat your pasta with the sauce.

6. If you are not serving the pasta immediately, then you can cover the pasta and refrigerate. Mix the bacon bits in before serving.

Herbes de Provence

Herbes de Provence is a spice blend that is from the Provence region of southeastern France.

Ingredients

- 2 tbsps. dried savory

- 1 tbsp. dried basil

- 1 tbsp. dried tarragon

- 1 tbsp. dried thyme

- 1 tbsp. dried rosemary

- 1 tbsp. dried marjoram

- 1 ½ tsps. dried lavender buds

Directions

1. Mix all together and use as desired. Store in a cool dry place.

Homemade Taco Seasoning

Homemade taco seasoning can be used to give a Mexican twist to your favorite dishes. You can also add it to sour cream for a garnish or dip.

Ingredients

- 2 tbsps. chili powder or cayenne pepper

- 2 tbsps. ground cumin

- 1 tbsp. garlic powder

- 1 tbsp. onion powder

- 1 tbsp. dried oregano

- 1 tbsp. sweet paprika

- ½ tsp. black pepper

Directions

1. Mix all together and use as desired. Store in a cool dry place.

Vegan Spicy Tomato Soup With Herby Pitas

Ingredients

For the soup:

- 2 tbsps. olive oil

- 1 large onion

- 1 large red pepper, chopped

- ½ tsp. salt

- 2 cloves garlic

- 1 jalapeño

- 1 (1-inch) piece ginger

- 2 tsps. ground coriander

- 1 tsp. ground cumin

- 2 ½ lbs. tomatoes, roughly chopped

- 2 ½ cups water

- 2 pocketless pitas

For the topping:

- 1 tbsp. brown sugar

- 2 tbsps. butter or olive oil

- 2 tbsps. finely shredded unsweetened coconut

- 2 tbsps. cilantro

Directions

1. Turn a large Dutch oven to medium-low. Put some olive oil into the pot. Once the olive oil is warm then you can add onion, red pepper, and salt. Cook until the onions and pepper are tender. This can take anywhere from 8–10 minutes.

2. While the onion and pepper are cooking in olive oil, grate the garlic, jalapeno, and ginger. Add to the onion and pepper mix. Stir well and cook for 1 minute to mix the flavors. Then add in ground coriander and ground cumin.

3. Add the tomatoes and water into the pot and increase the heat so that the soup can simmer while partially covered. Simmer for 10 minutes.

4. Toast your pitas while the tomatoes are cooking. You can toast them in the oven by turning on the grill or you can pop them into a toaster or toast them on a grill pan.

5. Once the tomato soup is cooked, allow it to cool for 15 minutes. The cooling time is especially necessary if you are going to use a blender instead of a hand blender. Pour the soup into your blender and puree until it is smooth. If you are using a hand blender, blend until smooth.

6. Whisk the brown sugar and olive oil or butter with finely shredded coconut and cilantro until combined fully.

7. Spread the brown sugar mix onto the pita and serve with the tomato soup.

Summer Pesto Pasta

Ingredients

- 16 oz. spaghetti

- 2 ears corn, shucked

- 1 medium yellow squash, cut into ½-inch-thick slices

- 1 medium zucchini, cut into ½-inch-thick slices

- 1 small bell pepper, seeded and cut into sixths

- 4 green onions, trimmed

- 2 tbsp. olive oil

- 1 lemon

- ½ cup store-bought refrigerated pesto

- 1 pint grape tomatoes, halved

- ¼ cup packed fresh parsley, chopped

Directions

1. Heat the grill to medium-high. Cook your spaghetti as per the manufacturer's instructions. Strain the spaghetti and

rinse with cold water before setting it into a bowl. Allow the spaghetti to cool completely.

2. Add the corn, squash, zucchini, bell pepper, and onions into a separate bowl.

3. Sprinkle the vegetables with oil and seasoning, and toss until the vegetables are well coated.

4. Place the vegetables into a baking tray and grill in stages. The total grilling time needed will be 10 minutes. You will need to grill the corn first as it needs all 10 minutes to cook.

5. When your corn has been in for 5 minutes, you can add the squash, zucchini, and bell pepper onto the baking tray.

6. Grill until there are grill marks on your vegetables. In the last 2 minutes, grill your onions.

7. Grate zest from the lemon and squeeze out about 2 tbsps. juice. Mix the zest and juice into pesto and add in seasoning.

8. Cube your squash, zucchini, bell pepper, and onions, or cut into whichever shapes you desire. Place into a bowl and add pesto. Last but not least, shuck the corn kernels from the cob.

9. Combine the rest of the ingredients together with the pesto and vegetables. Toss to coat and serve immediately.

Spring Minestrone Soup

Ingredients

- 2 tbsps. olive oil

- 1 medium leek, thinly sliced

- 2 medium carrots, chopped

- 8 sprigs of fresh thyme, tied together

- 3 large red potatoes, chopped

- 2 quarts low-sodium chicken or vegetable broth

- 1 bunch of asparagus, sliced

- 1 (15 oz.) can of navy beans, rinsed and drained (optional)

- 2 tbsps. chopped fresh dill

- ½ tsp. salt

- ½ tsp. pepper

Directions

1. Turn your stovetop to medium heat.

2. Take an 8-quart pot and add 2 tbsps. olive oil. Once the oil is warm, add in the leek, carrots, thyme, and about ¼ tsp. salt. Sauté for 8 minutes, stirring frequently so that the vegetables do not stick.

3. Once the vegetables are softened, add in chopped red potatoes and broth. Bring the soup to boil and cover.

4. Once the soup is brought to boil, lower the heat and allow it to simmer. Add asparagus. Simmer for approximately 25 minutes or until the potatoes are cooked through and are soft.

5. Once the potatoes are cooked through, search for the thyme and then discard it.

6. You can now stir in navy beans if you have them on hand. Alternately, you can stir in any other beans—experiment to your taste. Add fresh dill, ¼ tsp. salt, and ½ tsp. pepper to the soup and serve. Enjoy!

I hope that these recipes inspire you to take a culinary journey as well! I also hope that these recipes inspire you to try planting a wide variety of fruits, vegetables, herbs, and flowers. Gardens are the gifts you give to yourself that keep giving!

Conclusion

Raised beds are growing in popularity for all levels of gardeners. Regardless of whether you are a specialist, novice, senior resident, or even a kid, you can find how simple and advantageous it is to plant with a superb planter bed.

Beginners need to set up plenty of things for building up a new garden behind your home; however, it can likewise provide you with a lot of fun. If it is the first time you will going to develop a garden you should have a small one at first and afterward you can grow it in the later season which likewise comprises of vegetable gardens for beginners, vegetable gardening for beginners.

When you raise the bed of your planting surface you achieve a few things. Getting a planting surface lifted for a senior citizen is often the difference between them making the most of their lifelong quest for flowers or vegetable planting. This is likewise regularly helpful in mitigating back and neck strain that can get intolerable in older individuals. By raising the grower to eye level and a safe distance you are carrying the nursery to where it is agreeable for you. For kids and even learner nursery workers, lifting the bed considers a controlled area that is easily maintained. Rather than having an overwhelming area that can quickly get out of control, you have a smaller space that requires less weeding and pruning. Expert gardeners love the common sense of raised bed cultivating. At the point when the depth of the territory is extended by lifting it, you create an environment where the soil remains loose and deep, rather than compacted. Plants prefer this kind of condition and will prosper by having the option to sink their roots deep into the ground.

Also, many planting beds are being made of reused materials and wooden materials that are resistant to insects. This makes organic gardening a realistic possibility at your home no matter your skill level. So, there you have it. Everything you wanted to know about getting into raised bed gardens is now in your hand. It is my hope that this book has helped to answer many of the questions you had about starting your own raised bed garden. From why you would want to start one through to how it's done and how it is maintained, my goal has been to give you the information you need to get started. But that has only been half of my goal.

Giving you the information you need to get started is important but I have tried my best to stress the importance of researching your plants and listening to your garden. Taking the time to spend a few minutes every day with your garden will let you gather firsthand experience of what you would learn from a year of studying. Reading how it is done in a book is one thing but actually getting your hands dirty and learning to listen to your plants will take time and effort. It might sound like a lot of work but once you get into a flow of things, it is easy to lose track of how much time you are spending in your garden. It becomes such a peaceful hobby.

But it is also so rewarding. Watching the way your plants grow and thrive due to the careful consideration you have taken in setting up their raised bed home is a truly magical experience. Whether you are growing for beauty, consumption, or profit, you will find that the best part of the whole project is spending time with your plants and learning how they grow and communicate with us, their environment, and each other.

I hope that this book has left you with plenty of new questions and lots of ideas for how you could create wonderful raised bed gardens of your own. Make sure you take lots of photos to share the beautiful designs you've come up with so that you can inspire others to take up raised bed gardening themselves.

Made in the USA
Monee, IL
23 January 2022